BERNADINE

HOW TO FEED
Your Family
FOR £5 A DAY

MIX
Paper from
responsible sources
FSC C007454

FSC is a non-profit making organisation established to promote
the responsible management of the world's forests. Products carrying
the FSC label are independently certified to assure consumers that they co
from forests that are managed to meet the social, economic and
ecological needs of present and future generations,
and other controlled sources.

Find out more about HarperCollins and the environment at
www.harpercollins.co.uk/green

HARPER

To me mam, Agnes, whose Apple and Cheddar Cheese Pie will always be an inspiration to me.

HARPER

An imprint of HarperCollinsPublishers
77–85 Fulham Palace Road,
Hammersmith, London W6 8JB

www.harpercollins.co.uk

First published by Harper Thorsons as
How to Feed Your Family for £4 a Day, 1989.
This updated edition published 2012.

1 3 5 7 9 10 8 6 4 2

Text © Bernadine Lawrence 2012
Illustrations © Shutterstock/HarperCollins Design

Bernadine Lawrence asserts the moral right to
be identified as the author of this work

A catalogue record of this book is available from the British Library

ISBN 978-0-00-748565-9

Printed and bound in Great Britain by
Clays Ltd, St Ives plc

CONTENTS

CONTENTS

INTRODUCTION

'Ten years ago I had to dismiss my chauffeur and sell my Bentley after a failed business venture. Often it is the loss of a status symbol which causes shame and a feeling of worthlessness. But it can mean the start of a new venture in life, the beginning of self-discovery where you find you have to get your priorities sorted out and when hidden strengths and talents start to emerge out of necessity. Necessity is the mother of invention. Business failure can sometimes be a blessing in disguise.

I was used to spending £150 a week on food, drawing up outside restaurants, buying lots of take-aways and my bread from specialist food shops. After my income dropped dramatically I had to learn very quickly how to manage on a pittance. I was fearful of the future and dreaded those quarterly bills. I just did not see how I could possibly manage, and at first couldn't — I was sinking quickly into debt and even running out of food at the end of the week.

In order to manage I allowed myself just £4 a day to feed my family and buy household goods. I started cooking and experimenting with ingredients, trying to reproduce many of the meals I had enjoyed in vegetarian restaurants, and found I could produce delicious meals which were nutritionally excellent and cost very little. So we were eating a superior diet at minimum cost, and as the number of my recipes grew we found we were actually eating better than before ...'

Strange to think I wrote that back in 1991, and even stranger to go back all those years when I bought my first car – a 1950s Bentley MK VI, the most voluptuous car I'd ever seen.

So much has changed since then – the children have grown up, as children always do all too quickly before your eyes, and I am now a grandmother!

Mind you, I don't feel it and am grateful to be fit enough to run around and play boisterous games with my grandchildren, which I put down to my good diet and genes. I've always been fascinated by the nutrients nature has provided to help us stay healthy and youthful and which you can easily find at your local greengrocer.

There's a Victorian saying, 'The healthiest feast costs the least', and it still rings true today. In order to stay within budget, it's necessary to eat less red meat and more beans and pulses, which turns out to be healthier anyway. I know it's incredible but after all these years, it's still possible to feed a family of four a healthy diet for just £5 a day. This is because, fortunately, the cost of its staple ingredients – wholegrains, beans, pulses and chicken – has not risen sharply, and let's pray it continues to stay that way in the face of rising food prices and increasing global food insecurity.

One key approach that can help you stay within budget is to plan meals as a weekly whole, rather than on a daily basis, so a week's worth of meals can be made from one main ingredient. For example, a pot roast can become sandwiches, pies, stews, stir-fries and soups. Another, of course, is eating seasonal produce, which tends to be cheaper and fresher than produce bought out of season.

In order to keep within budget, I try not to waste food or throw it away, and turn leftover ingredients into meals. 'Wilful waste makes woeful want' after all, and food waste is a major global issue.

This updated edition of *How to Feed Your Family for £5 a Day* is even better than before, and not just because of the new, mouthwatering and simple-to-follow recipes. More than that, these recipes are based on a diet which is sustainable – better for the planet, better for the body and better for the purse, and they all use ingredients that are a cinch to get hold of.

Also included to help you avoid overspending is my Good Budget Guide, which includes Top Shopping Tips, a Seasonal Food Calendar, Uses for Leftover Ingredients and tried-and-tested advice to show you how to eat better and save money.

Enjoy!

MEASURING GUIDE

The most accurate way of measuring with a spoon is to use level measures; that is, level off the top of the spoon with a knife. (A heaped spoon can contain anything from two to four times as much as a level spoon.)

Spoon Measurements

1 teaspoon = 5ml

2 teaspoons = 10ml/1 dessertspoon

3 teaspoons = 15ml/1 tablespoon

1 tablespoon = 15ml

1 level tablespoon sugar = 28g

1 heaped tablespoon flour = 28g

STORE CUPBOARD

With a well-stocked store cupboard you can knock up a quick meal at any time with just leftover ingredients. It's like having a meal for nothing!

Tinned Food

Fish
Tuna, sardines, salmon and mackerel are all rich in Omega 3 and 6. Great for tuna pasta, sardines on toast, fish cakes and salmon salad.

Beans
As well as baked beans, try red kidney beans for quick chilli con carne, butter beans in casseroles and chickpeas in curries and fresh houmous.

Tomatoes
Plum tomatoes, chopped and unchopped, are perfect for tomato-based sauces, pizza toppings, salsa, bolognese sauce and Neapolitan sauce.

Tomato purée
This is wonderful used in pizza toppings, tomato sauces, soups and casseroles.

Sweetcorn
Natural sweetcorn with only water added is perfect in pasta, salads or soups, or with tuna and mayonnaise in sandwiches or jacket potatoes.

Dry Food

Flour
Plain wholemeal flour is great for bread, pastry, crumble toppings and pancakes. Plain white flour can be used for sauces, cakes and for mixing with wholemeal flour.

Beans

Red kidney beans work well in chillies and salads. Black-eyed beans complement rice and peas. Butter beans are delicious in curries and stews. Mung beans are perfect in soups and for making home-sprouted beans.

Pulses

Green lentils/brown lentils taste great in pies, stews, curries, loaves and burgers. Red split lentils are so versatile and can be used in flans, pies, soups, stews, curries, loaves and burgers.

Sugar

Soft light brown sugar is best for cakes and crumble toppings.

Rice

Brown rice is packed with B vitamins and fibre.

Pasta

Wholewheat pasta is more nutritious than white pasta, and great for a quick meal.

Popcorn

Fast, healthy and delicious, popcorn is a great treat for kids.

Dried fruit

Raisins, currants, sultanas, apricots – add them to muesli, cakes and biscuits.

Spices / Condiments

Dried yeast to make your own bread.

Baking powder for cakes and biscuits.

Curry powder to make your own vegetable, fish, chicken or meat curries. Use in marinades and sauces.

Dried chillies are handy for spicing up meals.

Turmeric gives food a lovely flavour and yellow colour, and complements chicken.

Paprika is great in sauces, stews and marinades, and complements other spices.

Whole black peppercorns for freshly ground black pepper.

Coarse sea salt enhances flavours.

Nutmeg, whole cloves, cinnamon and *ginger* go well with sweet or savoury food.

Dried herbs such as parsley, sage, mint, basil and dill, for flavouring food with ease.

Jars / Bottles

Honey is great with pancakes, yoghurt, muesli, marinades, cakes and sauces.

Wholefruit jam – try it with pancakes and ice cream.

Peanut butter – try it with banana on toasted wholemeal butties, in satay sauce, stir-fries, smoothies, biscuits and crumble toppings.

Marmite or *Vegemite* are both great for making stocks, go nicely with tomato purée, work well in soups, casseroles, stews, curries, sauces, marinades and bastes, and (last but not least) are great on toast.

English mustard is delicious in dressings and marinades, and with roast meat and grills.

Olive oil – sauté or roast vegetables in olive oil and then add the oil to salad dressings and marinades.

Sunflower oil is lovely and light, perfect for cooking with, and for using in salad dressings and flan pastry.

Vinegar – malt, cider, wine and balsamic are all good in dressings, sauces and marinades.

Soy sauce is handy for seasoning stir-fries, stews, casseroles, soups and marinades.

Ketchup can be used to make delicious sauces and marinades, and children love it.

Salad cream – children love it on salad, especially with cucumber, or blended with tinned tuna or salmon for sandwich fillings and pasta dishes.

Fridge

Meat
Keep raw meat, poultry or chicken well wrapped and in the bottom part of the fridge where it is coolest.

Milk
Full-fat organic milk is rich in Omega 3. Soy milk is a good alternative.

Margarine
Sunflower margarine is high in polyunsaturates and is good in crumbles.

Cheese
Cheddar is handy for pizzas, quiches, flans, baked potatoes and pasta dishes.

Yoghurt
Natural and Greek yoghurt are both great in dressings, marinades, sauces and muesli.

Eggs
Use free-range whenever possible, especially for quiches, omelettes, stir-fries, cakes and Yorkshire puddings.

Salad
Lettuce, cucumber, tomatoes, spring onions and mushrooms, to garnish.

Vegetables
Carrots, broccoli, spinach, cauliflower and leeks are good for quick meals.

Fruit
Apples, pears, lemons and limes are delicious in fruit salads, dressings and puddings.

HINTS, TIPS & SUGGESTIONS

On buying vegetables

When buying vegetables, see that the green ones are crisp and a fresh green colour, not yellow. Root vegetables should be firm and not coarse. Tomatoes should be firm and red, but if bought a little green can be ripened in a dark drawer. Potatoes should be firm and have no shoots. Lettuce and other salad vegetables should be crisp, not limp.

On cooking vegetables

Most vegetables should be cooked in a small amount of water and covered while cooking. When cooking frozen peas add 1 tablespoon of cold water to 500g peas with a knob of butter and a pinch of salt. Double the amount of water when cooking fresh peas. Cover the peas and cook on a very low heat, stirring occasionally, for about 5–10 minutes.

Greens can be shredded and cooked with 4 tablespoons of water for 500g, a knob of butter and a pinch of salt. Cook until just tender but not soggy.

Spinach should not be shredded but covered and cooked with a drop of water and a knob of butter and seasoned to taste with salt and pepper. Cook on a low heat for 3–5 minutes.

Once the vegetables are cooked, drain them and save the liquid for stocks and soups.

On fan ovens

If the recipe you are following involves oven cooking and you have a fan oven, reduce the oven temperature by 20°C (68°F).

A NOTE ABOUT SHOPPING

An important tip to remember is to keep a 'shopping purse', that is, a purse used strictly for your weekly groceries. Say you want to allow yourself £33 for the week, put that amount in your purse at the beginning of the week. That way you can easily tell if you are keeping within budget.

Should you overshoot your weekly target in the beginning, this need not mean a failure to budget successfully; your weekly budget will gradually balance out.

A good way to keep within budget is to use up any ingredients you may already have in. This method is particularly useful towards the end of the week when you can use up ingredients in soups and stews.

TIPS FOR BUYING FOR ❙ OR ❙❙

Obviously single people and couples can make great use of this book.

Most of the ingredients in the recipes can be divided more or less by two, and surpluses can be chilled or frozen for future use.

It is not advisable to buy large quantities of highly perishable foods. These should be bought daily or every other day.

○ ○ ○ ○ ○ ○ ○ ○ ○ ○ ○ ○ ○ ○ ○ ○ ○ ○ ○

A TYPICAL WEEKLY SHOPPING LIST

1 small roasting chicken
2 x 1.5kg plain wholemeal flour
1.5kg plain white flour
2 large tins of baked beans
2 x 400g tins of tomatoes
1kg porridge oats
500g raisins
500g red split lentils
500g wholewheat spaghetti
500g black-eyed beans
2 x 500g sunflower margarine
1 litre sunflower oil
2 tins of tuna
1 jar Marmite or Vegemite
115g houmous
700g Cheddar cheese
2 mackerel
900g frozen peas
5 litres milk

12 eggs
500g lean minced beef
5kg potatoes
1 small red cabbage
900g onions
450g carrots
1 head of broccoli
1 green pepper
garlic
120g mushrooms
1 cucumber
4 lemons
3 lettuces
600g tomatoes
1 bunch of bananas
900g apples
450g pears
12 oranges

BREAKFASTS

Perfect Creamy Porridge
Feeds 4

115g porridge oats
850ml milk (whole, skimmed or soy)
4 tsp soft light brown sugar, for sprinkling
1 tsp ground cinnamon, for sprinkling

Method
1. Bring the oats and milk to the boil in a large saucepan, stirring with a wooden spoon. Reduce the heat and simmer for 3–5 minutes, stirring continually, until creamy.
2. Serve sprinkled with the sugar and ground cinnamon.

— ALTERNATIVELY —

○ Be indulgent and cook with a knob of butter or add cream.
○ Simmer with chopped banana and raisins.
○ Top with stewed fruit – try apples, pears, plums or rhubarb.
○ Top with fresh berries, grated apple, sliced strawberries or prunes.
○ For a crunchy topping, add roasted sunflower seeds or chopped walnuts.

Chocolate Porridge

○ Add 2 tablespoons of cocoa powder or 100g of Fairtrade chocolate
to the milk and sweeten to taste.

Toasted Oats with Raisins, Bananas and Strawberries

Feeds 4. Serve with milk or yoghurt

200g rolled oats
100g raisins
2 bananas, sliced
50g strawberries, sliced
caster sugar, for sprinkling, or runny honey, for drizzling

Method

1. Toast the oats in a large frying pan over a high heat for 3–5
   minutes until browned.
2. Mix the toasted oats, raisins, bananas and strawberries in a large
   bowl then divide into 4 bowls and sprinkle each with sugar or
   drizzle with honey, as desired.

– ALTERNATIVELY –

° Add different fruits according to what is in season, such as blackberries, mulberries or grated apple, or chopped nuts, dates and prunes.

....

Golden Apricot Granola

Feeds 6–8. Serve with fruit and milk or yoghurt

2 tbsp runny honey
2 tbsp soft light brown sugar
juice of half a lemon
100ml sunflower oil
300g large rolled oats
55g sunflower seeds
55g chopped hazelnuts
4 tbsp sesame seeds
55g sultanas
55g dried apricots, chopped
pinch of salt

Method

1. Preheat the oven to 150°C (300°F), Gas 2. Place the honey, sugar and lemon juice in a large bowl and blend.
2. Gradually mix in the sunflower oil and then the dry ingredients until they are all coated.
3. Spread the mixture into 2 baking trays lined with baking paper.
4. Bake in the oven, stirring frequently, for 45–60 minutes until golden and crispy.
5. Remove the trays from the oven and allow the mixture to cool for about 40 minutes. When cool, break into lumps and store in an airtight container until ready to serve.

Peanut Butter and Date Granola

Feeds 4. Serve with fruit and milk or yoghurt

4 tbsp runny honey
100ml sunflower oil
115g crunchy peanut butter
300g large rolled oats
55g seedless raisins
55g chopped dates

Method

1. Preheat the oven to 150°C (300°F), Gas 2. Place the honey, sunflower oil and peanut butter in a large pan and warm over a low heat until the peanut butter has just melted and all the ingredients are starting to blend, then remove from the heat.
2. Add the dry ingredients and mix until fully coated.
3. Spread the mixture into 2 baking trays lined with baking paper.
4. Bake in the oven, stirring frequently, for 45–60 minutes until golden and crispy.
5. Remove the trays from the oven and allow the mixture to cool for about 40 minutes. When cool, break into lumps and store in an airtight container until ready to serve.

Popcorn for Breakfast

*Feeds 4–6. A cheaper and healthier alternative to puffed rice
or wheat breakfast cereals, popcorn contains no preservatives,
sugar or salt (until you put it in there yourself)*

3 tbsp sunflower oil
3 tbsp popping corn
570ml milk
4 tsp soft light brown sugar or 1 tbsp runny honey

Method

1. Heat the oil in a large pan over a high heat for 1–2 minutes until just starting to spit. Add the popping corn and cover the pan with a tight-fitting lid, then reduce the heat. The corn will start to pop as it cooks.
2. When the popping sounds slow down to about 3–4 seconds apart, the popcorn is ready.
3. Divide into bowls, add milk and sweeten to taste with sugar or honey.

Fruit and Nut Breakfast Trail Mix

Feeds 6–8. Serve with milk or yoghurt if preferred

60g popped popcorn
140g raisins
2 tbsp sunflower seeds
2–3 tbsp runny honey
3 tbsp crunchy peanut butter
1 tbsp tahini
2–3 tbsp sunflower oil

Method

1. Put the popcorn, raisins and sunflower seeds in a large bowl and set aside.
2. Melt the honey, peanut butter, tahini and oil in a saucepan over a medium heat, stirring with a wooden spoon.
3. Add the mixture to the popcorn, raisins and sunflower seeds. Mix well and serve. Great for snacks, too.

Honey Polenta

Feeds 4. Serve with butter, jam or cottage cheese. Also works well with fruit and spices such as cinnamon or nutmeg

1 litre milk
115g fine polenta
1 tbsp runny honey or brown sugar, to taste

Method

1. In a large saucepan, stir the milk gradually into the polenta with a wooden spoon.

2. Bring to the boil, then reduce the heat and simmer gently for 10 minutes, stirring constantly.
3. Sweeten to taste with the honey or brown sugar and serve.

– ALTERNATIVELY –

° For a thicker, more pudding-like consistency, use only 850ml of milk.

....

Breakfast Corncake Stack

Makes 16 corncakes. Serve with cottage cheese and honey
or sliced peaches and crème fraîche

2 eggs
300ml milk
115g fine polenta
pinch of salt
1–2 tbsp melted butter or sunflower oil

Method

1. In a large bowl, beat the eggs well with a fork. Gradually add the milk, polenta and salt until you have a batter the consistency of double cream.
2. Heat the butter or oil in a large frying pan and drop the batter by spoonfuls into the hot pan.
3. Fry for 2–3 minutes, turning once, until golden brown.

Grilled Banana Split

Feeds 4. A healthy alternative to the cream-filled classic

4 bananas
dollop of jam or honey
chopped nuts, for sprinkling
2 tbsp yoghurt

Method

1. Make a slit in each banana skin from end to end. Place under the grill at a medium heat for 10 minutes.
2. Split open the skins and serve the bananas in their peel with jam or honey, a sprinkling of chopped nuts and yoghurt.

....

Golden Banana Fritters

Feeds 4

1–2 tbsp sunflower oil
4 bananas, peeled and chopped into 3 pieces each
400ml of Coating Batter (see page 144)
1–2 tbsp runny honey or maple syrup

Method

1. Heat the oil in a large frying pan until hot, then dip each piece of banana in the coating batter.
2. Fry in the pan for 2–3 minutes, turning with a spatula, until golden brown.
3. Drain on kitchen paper and serve hot, drizzled with honey or maple syrup.

Healthy Honey-Yoghurt Sundae

Feeds 4. Great for using up overripe fruit

300g yoghurt
1 tbsp runny honey
1 tbsp currants, raisins or sultanas
1 tbsp porridge oats
150g ripe strawberries

Method

Mix together all the ingredients and serve.

– ALTERNATIVELY –

° Try with bananas, peaches or seedless grapes.

....

Fruity Pancakes

Feeds 4

a stack of 8 Pancakes (see page 143)
an assortment of sliced fruit to fill them with

These are some of my favourites:
° Honey, lemon juice and banana
° Strawberries and cream
° Peaches, honey and yoghurt
° Raspberry purée

LIGHT MEALS AND SNACKS

Warming Cheesy Rice Bake

Feeds 4

You will need an ovenproof pie dish approximately 14 x 18cm

350g cooked rice (140g uncooked rice cooked according
    to packet instructions)
225g strong Cheddar, grated
150ml milk or stock made from boiled water mixed with
    1 tbsp Marmite or Vegemite
30–60g butter or margarine
sea salt and freshly ground black pepper

Method
1. Preheat the oven to 170°C (325°F), Gas 3. Layer the cooked rice
   and the grated cheese in the pie dish (starting and ending with
   rice), lightly seasoning with salt and pepper and adding a little
   milk or stock to each layer as you go. Feel free at this stage to add

any cooked beans, vegetables, meat or fish – this is a chance to use up perfectly good leftovers.
2. Dot with knobs of butter and bake for 20–30 minutes until golden brown.

....

Crispy Potato Fritters
Makes 16–18. Feeds 4

900g potatoes, mashed (for a reminder of how to make mashed potato, see Buttery Mash on page 135 but don't add butter or seasoning)
2 tbsp breadcrumbs
5 eggs
2 tsp tomato purée
3 garlic cloves, crushed and finely chopped
3–4 tbsp vegetable oil
sea salt and freshly ground black pepper

Method
1. Mix together all the ingredients except the oil and season with salt and pepper.
2. Heat the oil in a large frying pan and when hot, drop tablespoons of the mixture into the pan and cook until brown on both sides, turning once.

....

Sliced Potatoes and Crispy Bacon in Rich White Sauce
Feeds 4

900g potatoes, scrubbed or peeled, as preferred
2 tbsp vegetable oil
55–85g streaky bacon, cubed

1 large onion, finely chopped
2 level tbsp plain white flour
570ml milk
a little freshly grated nutmeg
sea salt and freshly ground black pepper

Method

1. Cut the potatoes in half and place in a large saucepan. Cover in cold water and bring to the boil, then reduce the heat and simmer gently for about 15 minutes until tender. Cut one of the larger pieces in half to check it is cooked through.
2. While the potatoes are boiling, heat the oil in a large pan. Add the bacon and fry for 3–5 minutes over a medium heat. Add the onion, stir and continue to cook for another 3–5 minutes until the onion is golden.
3. Sprinkle over the flour and gradually add the milk. Stir well, grate in some nutmeg to taste, and simmer gently for 5 minutes.
4. Drain and cut the potatoes into 2–3cm thick slices while they are still hot.
5. Season the potatoes with salt and pepper then add to the sauce. Stir and simmer together for 5–10 minutes. Serve immediately.

*****

Stuffed Potatoes

Feeds 4

4 medium-size baked potatoes (see steps 1–2 of Jacket Potatoes on page 133)
60g butter
sea salt and freshly ground black pepper

Method

1. Split the baked potatoes in half and scoop the cooked potato out of the skins and into a bowl. Season with salt and pepper and combine with the butter until golden.
2. Fill the skins with the potato mixture.

– ALTERNATIVELY –

If preferred, add any of these fillings to the mixture before replacing in the skins:

° 200g Cheddar cheese, grated
° 400g tin of red kidney beans, drained; 100g Cheddar cheese, grated; 1 tbsp tomato purée
° 100g Cheddar cheese, grated; 100g bacon, chopped and fried
° Cooked kipper fillets (you can find boil-in-the-bag kippers in most major supermarkets); melted butter; juice of half a lemon; ½–1 tsp chilli flakes
° 2 tins of tuna, drained; 2 tbsp Greek yoghurt
° 200g cream cheese; 70g smoked salmon pieces

Corn on the Cob

Feeds 4

4 sweetcorn cobs
4 knobs of butter
sea salt and freshly ground black pepper

Method

1. If you're using corn in silks, shuck the corn by removing the leafy wrapping and the thready corn silks and wash the cobs.
2. Drop in boiling water and cook for 10–15 minutes.

Alternatively, boil in milk and water using ordinary or powdered milk. This makes the corn slightly sweeter.
3. Serve hot with butter, salt and pepper.

– ALTERNATIVELY –

Baked Corn on the Cob

For corn cobs in husks

1. If you're able to get hold of corn on the cob still in its husk, keep the leaves on to retain moisture and bake for 15–20 minutes in a preheated oven at 180°C (350°F), Gas 4. When the outer leaves are beginning to turn brown, it's ready.
2. Peel back the husks or just pull them off. Pull the silks off the end and serve.

For corn cobs not in husks

If you aren't able to get hold of corn in husks, just wrap the cobs individually in foil, twisting the ends, and bake in a preheated oven for 25 minutes at 200°C (400°F), Gas 6.

Tip

To remove corn kernels (cooked or raw) from the cob, stand the corn upright in a wide bowl and, holding the upper end, cut downwards along the cob. Perfect for soups, salads and pies.

Spicy Winter Bean Stew

Feeds 4. Delicious with Corn on the Cob (see page 27)

2 tbsp vegetable oil
1–2 onions, sliced
1–2 garlic cloves, crushed

400g tin of red kidney beans, with their water
400g tin of chopped tomatoes
1 tbsp soy sauce
1 tsp Marmite or Vegemite
1 tbsp tomato purée
½ tsp chilli flakes
sea salt and freshly ground black pepper

Method

1. Heat the oil in a large pan and fry the onions and garlic until soft.
2. Add the rest of the ingredients and simmer, stirring occasionally, for 15–20 minutes.

....

Filled Omelettes

Feeds 4. Makes 1 large omelette.

Method

1. Choose and prepare one of the fillings from the following suggestions for your omelette, or invent your own.
2. Follow steps 1–3 of the basic Omelette recipe (see page 152), then add the filling.
3. Wait a few seconds for the mixture to set slightly, then draw the edges into the centre so the uncooked egg can run into the space. Leave to cook for 3–5 minutes on a medium heat until soft or set.
4. Serve flat or fold over a third of your omelette into the centre, then fold over the opposite third. Turn out onto a warm plate.

Chinese omelette

Stir-fry 4 small sliced onions with 60g of beansprouts in a large frying pan for 5–10 minutes. Add 150g of diced or shredded ham or leftover roast chicken with 1 tablespoon of soy sauce and season to taste with salt and black pepper, then stir-fry for a further 5 minutes.

Crispy bacon and potato omelette

Boil 3 medium potatoes for 15 minutes until tender and fry 1 or 2 rashers of bacon for 2–5 minutes until crisp. Dice both. Leave the omelette to cook until soft on top, then turn the omelette over with a spatula and brown the other side. Serve flat.

Cheese omelette

Use 60g of grated or diced cheese – Cheddar, goat's cheese, Emmental and Manchego all work well. Cook the omelette until set, fold in thirds and serve.

Ham and onion omelette

Fry 50g of chopped ham and 1 small finely chopped onion for 5 minutes until soft. Cook the omelette until set.

Omelette with sautéed mushrooms

Fry 50g of sliced button or chestnut mushrooms in a knob of butter, and add just before the omelette sets.

Omelette aux fines herbs

Add 1 tablespoon of finely chopped herbs, such as parsley and chives, or 1 teaspoon of dried mixed herbs.

Prawn omelette

Pan-fry 50g of pre-cooked prawns or shrimps for 2 minutes, then add to the omelette before folding. Remember to defrost pre-cooked frozen prawns completely before cooking by wrapping in cling film and placing in a sink of cold water for about an hour.

Omelette with flaked fish

Use 50g cooked, flaked fish, fresh or tinned – salmon, tuna and mackerel all work well, depending on your personal preference. Add to the omelette just before folding.

Farmhouse Cheese and Potato Cakes

Makes 12–16. Feeds 4 as a snack or as part of a main meal

500g potatoes, mashed with butter (for a reminder of how to make
    mashed potato, see Buttery Mash on page 135)
200g grated Cheddar cheese
1 tsp chopped chives
2 eggs, beaten
plain white flour, for dusting
2 tbsp breadcrumbs, spread out on a plate
sea salt and freshly ground black pepper

Method

1. Preheat the oven to 190°C (375°F), Gas 5. Set aside a little of the
   beaten egg for brushing.
2. Place the potatoes, cheese, chives and the remaining beaten
   egg in a large bowl, season with salt and pepper and then mix
   to form a dough.
3. Turn out onto a lightly floured surface and roll into a wide sausage
   shape. Cut the sausage of dough into 12–16 small slices and shape
   into cakes.
4. Brush with the beaten egg you set aside earlier, and then roll the
   cakes in the breadcrumbs until evenly coated on all sides. These
   cakes can be refrigerated until ready to cook.
5. Place in a roasting tin and bake in the oven for 20–30 minutes,
   or alternatively fry in vegetable or sunflower oil on both sides
   until golden.

Scrambled Eggs with Smoked Salmon

Feeds 4

30g butter
6 eggs
1 tsp milk
1 tsp salt
60g smoked salmon pieces
sea salt and freshly ground black pepper

Method
1. See Scrambled Eggs (on page 151) but just before the eggs have set add the salmon and continue to stir until fluffy.

Savoury Bread and Cheese Pudding

*Feeds 4–6. A delicious way to use up
stale bread, and perfect comfort food*

You will need a 20 x 25cm shallow ovenproof dish

12 slices of wholemeal bread, buttered
225g cheese, grated (I find strong Cheddar does the trick)
3 eggs
425ml milk
1 tsp mustard
15g butter or margarine
sea salt and freshly ground black pepper

Method

1. Preheat the oven to 180°C (350°F), Gas 4. Alternate layers of bread and cheese, starting with bread and ending with cheese, in the ovenproof dish.
2. Beat the eggs, milk, mustard and seasoning together and pour over the bread and cheese. Ideally, let stand for 1–1½ hours.
3. Dot the top with knobs of butter or margarine and bake in the oven for 20 minutes until golden brown. Serve with salad.

SAVOURY PANCAKES

Baked Chicken or Flaked Fish and Mushroom Pancake Cannelloni

Fills 4–6 pancakes

You will need a 30 x 35cm baking dish

150g cooked chicken, shredded, or 150g cooked white fish fillets
    such as cod, haddock, coley or plaice, flaked
300ml Basic Béchamel Sauce (see page 146)
55g button or chestnut mushrooms, sautéed in a knob of butter
a stack of 4–6 Pancakes (see page 143)
sea salt and freshly ground black pepper

Method

1. Preheat the oven to 180°C (350°F), Gas 4 and grease your baking dish. Combine the chicken or fish with the sauce and the mushrooms, and season with salt and pepper.
2. Fill each pancake with 1 tablespoon of the mixture and roll each one up.
3. Lay them side by side in the baking dish and bake for 15 minutes.

33

Sautéed Mushroom, Onion and Beansprout Pancakes

Fills 4–6 pancakes

55g cup mushrooms, sliced
1 onion, sliced
115g beansprouts, chopped
1–2 tbsp vegetable oil
1 tbsp soy sauce
a stack of 4–6 Pancakes (see page 143)
freshly ground black pepper

Method
1. Sauté the vegetables in a little oil for 10 minutes.
2. Add the soy sauce, season with black pepper and divide the mixture between your pancakes. Roll and serve.

....

Sweetcorn and Cup Mushroom Pancakes

Fills 4–6 pancakes

1 onion, sliced
55g cup mushrooms, sliced
115g sweetcorn kernels (tinned, fresh or frozen)
1–2 tbsp vegetable oil
300ml Basic Béchamel Sauce (see page 146)
a stack of 4–6 Pancakes (see page 143)
salt and freshly ground black pepper

Method
1. Sauté the vegetables in a little oil for 10–15 minutes.
2. Add the béchamel sauce, season with salt and pepper and then divide the mixture between your pancakes. Roll and serve.

....

Cream Cheese and Wilted Spinach Pancakes
Fills 4–6 pancakes

1 onion, sliced
1 tbsp vegetable oil
225g spinach, shredded
115g cream cheese
a stack of 4–6 Pancakes (see page 143)

Method
1. Sauté the onion in oil for 5 minutes. Add the spinach and sauté for a further 5–10 minutes.
2. Remove from the heat and stir in the cream cheese. Divide the mixture between your pancakes, roll and serve.

TOAST AND SANDWICHES

Welsh Rarebit

Feeds 4

115g strong Cheddar cheese, grated
3 tbsp milk
15g butter or margarine
3 tbsp ale or stout (optional)
4–6 slices of toast (granary or wholemeal are traditional for this
    recipe, but you can use whichever bread you prefer or have in)
sea salt and freshly ground black pepper

Method
1. Put the cheese, milk, butter, ale or stout (if using) and seasoning
   in a saucepan over a low heat, and allow the cheese to melt slowly.
2. Once the cheese has completely melted, pour the mixture over the
   toast and brown under the grill for 3–5 minutes until bubbling.

Gourmet Sardines on Toast

Feeds 4

120g tinned boneless sardines
1 tbsp milk or plain yoghurt
55g cheese, grated (any hard English cheese will do here
    – try Cheddar, Red Leicester or Double Gloucester)
4–6 slices of toast (granary or wholemeal), buttered
sea salt and freshly ground black pepper

Method

1. Mash the sardines with a fork, season with salt and pepper and combine with the milk or yoghurt and most of the cheese, keeping some aside for sprinkling on top.
2. Pile the mixture on the toast. Scatter over the remaining cheese and brown under the grill for 3–5 minutes.

Sandwich Suggestions

Everyone has their own idea of what constitutes the perfect sandwich, so I only provide some ideas to inspire, and leave it up to you to decide on quantities

- Taramasalata and salad
- Houmous spread and salad
- Mackerel pâté and salad
- Ham and salad
- Crab pâté and salad
- Chicken and salad
- Tuna and sweetcorn
- Smoked mackerel mashed with yoghurt, garnished with thinly sliced orange
- Tinned sardines mashed with yoghurt or salad cream
- Cottage cheese and olives
- Grated cheese, sliced onion, Greek yoghurt
- Hot or cold cooked beans with Marmite or Vegemite and herbs, and garnished with salad
- Marmite or Vegemite, cheese and salad
- Hard-boiled eggs and grated cheese combined with cream or yoghurt
- Hard-boiled eggs and salad with salad cream or yoghurt dressing
- Scrambled eggs on their own or with sweetcorn or mushrooms
- Toasted cheese sandwich with salad
- Baked beans on toast

SOUPS AND STOCK

How to make delicious soups, use up leftovers and save money:

Soup is great for using up any leftover vegetables, cooked meat, fish or beans. Keep cooked meat stored in the fridge in a sealed container and use within 3 days.

- Rice and pasta – either add cooked leftovers or cook the rice, pasta or noodles in the soup. Use small pasta shapes or break spaghetti into short pieces.
- The bones left over from a chicken or turkey make excellent stock. Simmer with any leftover vegetables such as carrots, onions and celery for 50–60 minutes in 300ml of water.
- A ham bone or chicken carcass, or bits of leftover ham, chicken and bacon make a good stock and go especially well with lentils.
- Leftover salad vegetables – thin slices of cucumber, pepper or chopped watercress make a great garnish.
- Grated cheese – Cheddar and Parmesan melt deliciously into hot

soups. Sprinkle on top just before serving.

○ Bacon – fry or grill until crisp. Sprinkle over soup for added flavour.

○ Herbs – chop finely or use sprigs as a garnish to liven up any soup.

○ Cream or yoghurt – swirling on top of soup just before serving makes soup look and taste good.

○ Croutons made from leftover bread – dice and fry in olive oil with crushed garlic until golden and crisp.

STOCK

If you are not using homemade stock immediately, allow it to cool, keep in plastic containers in the fridge for up to 3 days, or freeze the stock for up to 3 months in ice-cube trays so you can use as many or as few as you like when needed in soups, sauces, risottos, gravy, casseroles and pies.

Chicken Stock

Makes about 1 litre

a leftover roast chicken carcass
1 large onion, sliced
1 large carrot, chopped
2 celery sticks, chopped
1 bay leaf
sea salt and freshly ground black pepper

Method

1. Put the carcass with the skin and any meat into a large saucepan with the vegetables.
2. Cover with 2 litres of cold water, add the bay leaf and season with salt and pepper.

3. Bring to the boil, cover and simmer for 3 hours.
4. Remove and discard the carcass, bones and bay leaf and retain the vegetables and meat in the stock.
5. Alternatively strain the stock through a sieve and discard the vegetables and meat or store for use in another recipe.

....

Ham Stock

Makes about 1 litre

the bones and leftover meat of a cooked ham
2 carrots, chopped
2 onions, chopped
2 celery sticks, chopped
1 turnip, chopped
2 garlic cloves
2 tsp fresh mixed herbs
sea salt and freshly ground black pepper

Method
1. Place all the ingredients in a large saucepan with 2 litres of cold water. Bring to the boil, cover and simmer gently for 3 hours.
2. Remove the ham bone and discard, and leave the meat and vegetables in the stock
3. Alternatively strain the stock through a sieve and discard the vegetables and meat or store for use in another recipe.

Tomato Bouillon

Feeds 4

300g jar of tomato purée
850ml stock (boiled water mixed with 1 tbsp Marmite or Vegemite)
1 tsp brown sugar
flat-leaf parsley, finely chopped, for sprinkling
sea salt and freshly ground black pepper

Method

1. Bring the tomato purée and stock to the boil. Add the sugar and season to taste with salt and pepper.
2. Sprinkle with the chopped parsley and serve with toast.

....

Mulligatawny Soup

Feeds 4

300g uncooked red split lentils
1 tbsp curry powder
1 litre stock (boiled water mixed with 1 tbsp Marmite or Vegemite)
1 tbsp vegetable oil
2 carrots, grated
2 onions, sliced
1 apple, peeled, cored and chopped
garlic cloves, crushed, to taste
3 tbsp lemon juice
sea salt and freshly ground black pepper

Method

1. Put the lentils, curry powder and stock in a large saucepan and bring to the boil.

2. Meanwhile, heat the oil in a frying pan and sauté the carrots, onions, apple and garlic for 15 minutes.
3. Add the vegetables to the stock and simmer for 30 minutes. Season to taste with salt and pepper and stir in the lemon juice. Serve.

....

Minestrone

Feeds 4

1 litre stock (boiled water mixed with 1 tbsp Marmite or Vegemite)
55g wholewheat spaghetti, broken into small pieces
55g chopped bacon (optional)
115g porridge oats
115g cabbage, finely shredded
1 turnip, grated
1 onion, thinly sliced
1 tbsp vegetable oil
pinch of dried or freshly chopped thyme
sea salt and freshly ground black pepper

Method

1. Bring the stock to the boil in a large saucepan. Add the spaghetti and simmer gently.
2. Sauté the bacon, oats and vegetables in the oil for 15 minutes.
3. Add them to the stock along with the thyme and simmer gently for 30 minutes. Season to taste with salt and pepper. Serve.

Hearty Leek and Red Split Lentil Soup

*Feeds 4. Serve with wholemeal bread or dumplings (see the recipes
for Bargain Bread on page 120 and Butter Dumplings on page 130)*

3 carrots, grated
2 onions, sliced
2–3 garlic cloves, crushed
1 leek, chopped
1 tbsp vegetable oil
300g red split lentils, cooked in 1 litre of cold water as for use
     in soups (see Red Split Lentils on page 140)
1 tbsp soy sauce
1 tbsp tomato purée
sea salt and freshly ground black pepper

Method
1. Sauté the vegetables in the oil for 15 minutes then add them
   to the cooked lentils once they are simmering.
2. Add the soy sauce and tomato purée. Season with salt and
   pepper and simmer for 25 minutes. Serve.

....

Spring Vegetable Soup

Feeds 4

115g peas (fresh or frozen)
1 celery stick, chopped
1 young carrot, grated
1 onion, sliced
55g cup mushrooms, chopped

1 tbsp vegetable oil
850ml Basic Béchamel Soup Base (see page 145)
sea salt and freshly ground black pepper

Method

1. Sauté the vegetables in the oil for 15 minutes.
2. Add the vegetables and seasoning to the béchamel soup base. Simmer for 10–15 minutes, stirring occasionally. Serve.

....

Cream of Celery Soup

Feeds 4

6 celery sticks, chopped
1 onion, sliced
small bunch of flat-leaf parsley, finely chopped
1 tbsp vegetable oil
850ml Basic Béchamel Soup Base (see page 145)
sea salt and freshly ground black pepper

Method

1. Sauté the celery, onion and parsley in vegetable oil for 15 minutes.
2. Add the vegetables to your béchamel soup base, blitz in a blender until smooth if preferred, season with salt and pepper and simmer for 10–15 minutes. Serve.

Cream of Mushroom Soup

Feeds 4. Serve with wholemeal bread or dumplings (see the recipe
for Bargain Bread on page 120 and Butter Dumplings on page 130)

1 carrot, grated
1 onion, sliced
115g mushrooms, chopped (portobello mushrooms, preferably,
     but you can use whichever variety you prefer)
1 tbsp vegetable oil
850ml Basic Béchamel Soup Base (see page 145)
sea salt and freshly ground black pepper

Method

1. Sauté the carrot, onion and mushrooms in the vegetable oil for 15 minutes.
2. Add the vegetables to the béchamel soup base, blitz in a blender
    until smooth if preferred, season with salt and pepper and simmer
    for a further 10–15 minutes, stirring occasionally. Serve.

Mackerel and Mushroom Chowder

Feeds 4

1 carrot, grated
1 onion, sliced
1–2 garlic cloves, crushed
1 tbsp vegetable oil
1 small boneless mackerel (if using fresh mackerel, ask your
  fishmonger to clean, fillet and debone the fish, and peel off the
  skin before adding to the soup base)
55g button or chestnut mushrooms, sliced
2 tbsp flat-leaf parsley, finely chopped
850ml Basic Béchamel Soup Base (see page 145)
sea salt and freshly ground black pepper

Method

1. Sauté the carrot, onion and garlic in the oil for 10 minutes. Add the mackerel, cover and allow to cook for a further 5–10 minutes, stirring and turning the mackerel occasionally. Add the mushrooms and parsley.
2. Stir the cooked vegetables and fish into your soup base and season with salt and pepper. The fish should flake nicely and the soup turn golden. Alternatively you can blitz in a blender until smooth if preferred. Serve.

....

Roast Chicken and Chunky Vegetable Soup

Feeds 4. Perfect served with crusty bread (see Bargain Bread on page 120)

leftover roast chicken (a carcass with a bit of meat left on is ideal)
any leftover vegetables and juices from the roasting tin
3 cabbage leaves, finely shredded
2 carrots, sliced diagonally
1 onion, thinly sliced
3 garlic cloves, roughly chopped
100g cup mushrooms, chopped
any herb, roughly chopped (parsley, thyme and rosemary all complement roast chicken)
1 tsp Marmite or Vegemite
1 tbsp tomato purée
sea salt and freshly ground black pepper

Method

1. Put the roast chicken carcass, leftover roast vegetables, roasting juices, raw vegetables and herbs in a large saucepan and add 1.5 litres of cold water.

2. Bring to the boil, cover with the lid and simmer gently for 60 minutes.
3. Remove the carcass and bones from the soup, then add the Marmite or Vegemite and the tomato purée.
4. Season with salt and pepper and stir. Simmer gently for a further 30 minutes and serve. Tastes even better the next day!

– ALTERNATIVELY –

∘ Sauté the raw vegetables before adding to the soup.
∘ Great for using up other leftover vegetables including sweetcorn, peas, pepper and celery.

VEGETARIAN

Cheesy Sweet Potato and Bean Bake

Feeds 4

You will need a medium casserole dish

1 large onion, sliced
100g tomatoes, chopped
2 garlic cloves, thinly sliced
knob of butter or 1 tbsp vegetable oil
200g red kidney beans either cooked from dry
    (see Red Kidney Beans on page 138) or tinned, drained
200g sweet potatoes, boiled for 15 minutes in salted water and sliced
600ml Cheese Sauce (see page 147)

Method

1. Preheat the oven to 180°C (350°F), Gas 4. Sauté the onion, tomatoes and garlic for 5–10 minutes in butter or vegetable oil.
2. Layer a medium casserole dish first with the beans, then the onion, tomatoes and garlic mixture and finish with the sliced sweet potatoes.
3. Top with cheese sauce and bake for 30 minutes in the oven. Serve.

Layered Red Split Lentil, Spinach and Potato Casserole

Feeds 4

You will need a large casserole dish

2 red onions, sliced
2–3 garlic cloves, crushed and chopped
1–2 tbsp olive oil
200g spinach
340g red split lentils, cooked for use in flans and loaves
    (see Red Split Lentils on page 140), drained
juice of 2 limes
1 tbsp tomato purée
pinch of chilli flakes or chilli powder
6 medium potatoes, boiled for 10–15 minutes in salted water and sliced
100g butter or 115g grated hard cheese (such as Parmesan, Pecorino,
    Jarlsberg or Gruyère) or 300ml Cheese Sauce (see page 147)
sea salt and freshly ground black pepper

Method

1. Preheat oven to 180°C (350°F), Gas 4 and grease a large casserole dish.
2. Sauté the onion and garlic in the olive oil for 5 minutes and then remove from the heat.
3. Add the spinach and stir, then add the cooked, drained lentils,

which should be plump and firm, and stir with a wooden spoon.
4. Add the lime juice, tomato purée and chilli and stir. Season to taste with salt and pepper.
5. Layer your cooked ingredients in the casserole dish starting with the lentil and spinach mixture followed by the sliced potatoes. Repeat, ending with potatoes.
6. Dot with knobs of butter, or sprinkle with grated cheese, or top with cheese sauce.
7. Bake for 30–40 minutes or until golden brown.

....

Healthy Black-Eyed Beanburgers

Makes 10–12, feeds 4, sandwiched between wholemeal baps and served with Jacket Potatoes (see page 133) and Decadent Winter Slaw (see page 102)

300g black-eyed beans, either cooked from dry (see Black-Eyed Beans on page 139) or tinned, drained
2 small onions, chopped
3 garlic cloves, finely chopped
4 tbsp vegetable oil
170g sage and onion stuffing, prepared according to packet instructions
plain white flour, for shaping
sea salt and freshly ground black pepper

Method
1. Season the black-eyed beans.
2. Sauté the onions and garlic in 1 tablespoon of the oil and add them, with the stuffing, to the black-eyed beans.
3. Mash with a potato masher, then shape into 10–12 burgers and roll them in a little flour.
4. Leave to stand on a wire rack for 10 minutes, then either fry in the rest of the oil for about 10 minutes on each side until browned

or bake in a preheated oven at 200°C (400°F), Gas 6 in an oiled roasting tin for 10 minutes, turning once, until browned on both sides, and adding more oil if necessary.

Tip
Maximize oven use by baking potatoes on the top shelf of the oven while the burgers are cooking.

– ALTERNATIVELY –

Red Beanburgers

° Substitute the black-eyed beans for 300g of tinned or cooked dried red kidney beans (see Red Kidney Beans on page 138). Continue as for Black-Eyed Beanburgers.

....

Autumnal Black-Eyed Bean Stew with Dumplings
Feeds 4

150g black-eyed beans, either cooked from dry (see Black-Eyed
    Beans on page 139) or tinned, drained
2 tsp Marmite or Vegemite
450g potatoes, scrubbed or peeled and diced
1–2 tbsp vegetable oil
2 carrots, sliced
3 onions, sliced
2–3 garlic cloves, crushed
½ cucumber, chopped into large chunks
1 tbsp tomato purée
6 Butter Dumplings (see page 130)
sea salt and freshly ground black pepper

Method

1. Add the beans, Marmite or Vegemite and 1.5 litres of water to a large saucepan, bring to the boil and maintain for 5 minutes. Toss in the potatoes and continue to boil for a further 5 minutes, then cover and simmer for 10–15 minutes on the lowest heat.
2. While the beans and potatoes are simmering, sauté the vegetables in the oil for 10 minutes, starting with the carrots, then adding the onions and garlic, and ending with the cucumber. Add the vegetables to the beans and potatoes.
3. Add the tomato purée and season with salt and pepper.
4. Cover and simmer gently for 10–15 minutes. Add the dumplings, cover again and simmer for a further 10 minutes until the dumplings swell. Serve immediately.

– ALTERNATIVELY –

° Make a casserole – preheat the oven to 190°C (375°F), Gas 5.
° Continue as for Black-Eyed Bean Stew until the end of step 3.
° Place in a large casserole dish and bake for 30–40 minutes.
° Add the dumplings during the last 10 minutes of cooking.
° You can also replace the black-eyed beans with lentils for a tenderer stew with a nuttier flavour.

Cheddar and Sautéed Onion Quiche

Feeds 4. Serve with Jacket Potatoes (see page 133) and a green salad

1 Wholemeal Flan Pastry case, baked blind in a 22cm round flan tin,
4cm deep (see page 126)

Filling
3–4 onions, sliced
2–3 tbsp vegetable oil
225g Cheddar cheese, grated
3 eggs, beaten
sea salt and freshly ground black pepper

Method
1. Preheat the oven to 180°C (350°F), Gas 4. Sauté the onions
   in the oil over a low heat for 5–10 minutes, stirring regularly.
2. Remove from the heat and add the grated cheese and the eggs.
   Mix well, season with salt and pepper and turn into the pastry case.
3. Bake in the oven for 30–40 minutes until the filling is golden
   brown and firm.

....

One-Pot Pea and Potato Curry

Feeds 4 accompanied by Brown Rice (see page 137)

2 carrots, grated
1 celery stick, chopped
1 green pepper, deseeded and sliced
55g peas (fresh or frozen)
2–3 garlic cloves, crushed

4 small onions, sliced
2–3 tbsp vegetable oil
55g button mushrooms, sliced
3 medium potatoes, boiled for 15 minutes in salted water
400g tin of chopped tomatoes
5 tsp curry powder
2 tbsp soy sauce
1 tbsp tomato purée
squeeze of lemon juice
sea salt and freshly ground black pepper

Method
1. In a large pan sauté the carrots, celery, pepper, peas, garlic and onions in the oil for 10 minutes.
2. Add the mushrooms, stir then add the potatoes. Add the chopped tomatoes, stir in the curry powder and soy sauce and then season with salt and pepper.
3. Simmer gently for 30–40 minutes, add the tomato purée and a squeeze of lemon juice, stir and simmer for a further 10 minutes. Serve.

....

Wholemeal Cream Cheese and Vine Tomato Pizza

Feeds 4 as part of a main meal

Pizza Base
170g margarine or 3–4 tbsp vegetable oil
225g plain wholemeal flour
pinch of salt
olive oil, for brushing

Topping

3 tbsp tomato purée
1 tbsp cream cheese
3 garlic cloves, finely grated
1 onion, sliced (use white or red as preferred)
1 green pepper, deseeded and sliced
55g cup mushrooms, sliced
2 vine tomatoes, sliced
1 tsp chopped oregano or mixed herbs
olive oil, for drizzling
125g Cheddar cheese, grated
sea salt and freshly ground black pepper

Method

1. Preheat the oven to 190°C (375°F), Gas 5. To make the pizza base, either rub the margarine into the flour and salt until the mixture resembles fine breadcrumbs or, if using oil, mix the oil into the flour and salt with a knife. Add a little cold water (1 tablespoon if using margarine, 6 tablespoons if using oil) and knead into a dough.
2. Roll out the dough evenly on a floured surface into approximately a 25cm round, then transfer to a baking sheet and brush with a little olive oil. Combine the tomato purée and cream cheese and spread over the pizza base.
3. Sprinkle over the garlic then place the raw vegetables over the top, beginning with the onion and pepper, then followed by the mushrooms and vine tomatoes. Sprinkle with the herbs.
4. Drizzle with olive oil, top with the grated Cheddar and season with salt and pepper.
5. Bake in the middle of the oven for 20–25 minutes. Serve.

Spaghetti Neapolitan

Feeds 4

4 small onions, sliced
3 carrots, grated
1 green pepper, deseeded and chopped into chunks
55g button mushrooms
1–2 garlic cloves, crushed
1–2 tbsp vegetable oil
400g tin of chopped tomatoes
1 tbsp tomato purée
1 tsp mixed dried herbs
1 tbsp soy sauce
285g wholewheat spaghetti
sea salt and freshly ground black pepper

Method

1. Sauté the vegetables in oil in a large frying pan until just tender. Add the chopped tomatoes, tomato purée, herbs, soy sauce and seasoning.
2. Cover and simmer over a low heat for 30 minutes, stirring occasionally and adding a little water if the sauce becomes too thick.
3. When the sauce has been simmering for 15 minutes, lower the spaghetti into 1.75 litres of boiling salted water and simmer until just cooked – about 12 minutes – then drain. Toss together the sauce and the cooked spaghetti and serve.

Root Vegetable Pie

*Feeds 4 as part of a main meal
with a hearty salad*

1 Crumbly Pastry case, blind baked and lining a 24cm round pie dish,
5cm deep, with a third of the pastry left over for the lid (see steps 1–2
of Crumbly Pastry: Pie Case and Lid, page 127)

Filling

2 carrots, sliced
115g frozen peas
225g potatoes, boiled in salted water for 10 minutes and diced
2–3 tbsp vegetable oil
600ml Basic Béchamel Sauce (see page 146)
milk, for glazing
sea salt and freshly ground black pepper

Method

1. Preheat the oven to 170°C (325°F), Gas 3. Sauté the vegetables
   in the oil for 10 minutes over a medium heat, starting with the
   carrots, then adding the peas and boiled potatoes.
2. Stir in the béchamel sauce, season with salt and pepper, and fill
   your prepared pie case.
3. Roll out the rest of the pastry to make the lid (see steps 3–4
   of Crumbly Pastry: Pie Case and Lid on page 127 for a reminder
   of how to make a pie lid) and lay on top of the pie, pinching the
   edges together.
4. Once the uncooked pie has chilled in the fridge for 10 minutes, bake
   in the oven for 20–25 minutes until the pastry is golden brown.

Wilted Spinach, Potato and Sweetcorn Pie

Feeds 4

1 Crumbly Pastry case, blind baked and lining a 24cm round pie dish, 5cm deep, with a third of the pastry left over for the lid (see steps 1–2 of Crumbly Pastry: Pie Case and Lid, page 127)

Filling

4 small onions, sliced
1–2 tbsp vegetable oil
170g spinach, shredded
450g potatoes, boiled in salted water for 10 minutes and sliced or diced
100g sweetcorn (fresh or tinned)
600ml Cheese Sauce (see page 147)
milk, for glazing
sea salt and freshly ground black pepper

Method

1. Preheat the oven to 170°C (325°F), Gas 3.
2. While your pie case blind bakes, sauté the onions in the oil until golden – about 5 minutes. Stir in the spinach and sauté for a further 5 minutes.
3. After removing the blind-baked pie case from the oven, turn the temperature up to 180°C (350°F), Gas 4. Add the boiled potatoes and sweetcorn to the onion and spinach. Pour the cheese sauce over the vegetables, stir well for 5 minutes on a low heat, and season with salt and pepper.
4. Spoon the cheese and vegetable sauce into the pie case and top with a lid made from the remaining pastry (see steps 3–4 of Crumbly Pastry: Pie Case and Lid on page 127 for a reminder of how to make a pie lid).
5. After your uncooked pie has chilled in the fridge for 10 minutes, bake on the lowest shelf of the oven for 20 minutes, or until the pastry is golden brown.

Potato, Cheddar and Onion Tart with Spring Greens

Feeds 4

1 Wholemeal Flan Pastry case, baked blind in a 22cm round flan tin, 4cm deep (see page 126)

Filling
3–4 medium potatoes, scrubbed or peeled and diced
1–2 tbsp olive oil
30g butter
1 carrot, grated
250g spring greens, finely chopped
1 large onion, thinly sliced
drop of milk
200g Cheddar cheese, grated
sea salt and freshly ground black pepper

Method
1. Preheat the oven to 190°C (375°F), Gas 5. Fry the potatoes in the olive oil and butter in a large frying pan for 5 minutes on a medium-high heat. Reduce the heat, cover and allow to cook for a further 3–5 minutes.
2. Add the rest of the vegetables and a drop of milk and season to taste with salt and pepper, then cook uncovered on a low heat for 15–20 minutes, stirring regularly.
3. Add the grated cheese and stir well until the mixture has a nice dense consistency.
4. Pour your mixture into the prepared wholemeal pastry case and bake in the oven for 30–40 minutes until brown on top.

Sautéed Onion, Tomato and Red Split Lentil Tart

Feeds 6–8. Serve with boiled and buttered new potatoes and salad

1 Wholemeal Flan Pastry case, baked blind in a 22cm round flan tin, 4cm deep (see page 126)

Filling
250g red split lentils
1–2 tbsp vegetable oil
3–4 carrots, grated
4 small onions, sliced
2–3 garlic cloves, crushed
juice of 1–2 small lemons
2 tbsp tomato purée
chopped coriander leaves, cumin or paprika, to taste (optional)
115g strong Cheddar cheese, grated
sea salt and freshly ground black pepper

Method
1. Preheat the oven to 200°C (400°F), Gas 6. Bring the lentils and 430ml of cold water to the boil in a large uncovered saucepan, then reduce the heat and allow to simmer gently, stirring occasionally, for 15–25 minutes or until firm but tender and the liquid has reduced.
2. Meanwhile, heat the oil in a large frying pan and sauté the carrots, onions and garlic for 10–15 minutes until soft.
3. Add the vegetables to the cooked lentils along with the lemon juice and tomato purée and season with salt and pepper. If you want to give the flan a stronger flavour, also add some chopped coriander, cumin or paprika as desired. Stir well and spoon into the blind-

baked pastry case, then sprinkle over the grated cheese.
4. Bake in the oven for 20–25 minutes. The tart can be reheated once cool, and will keep in the fridge for 2 days. Prepare in advance for lunch the following day.

....

Rustic Kidney Bean, Green Pepper and Mushroom Goulash

Feeds 4. Delicious over jacket potatoes or brown rice (see page 133 for a flawless Jacket Potato and page 138 for Perfect Brown Rice)

4 onions, sliced
1 green pepper, deseeded and sliced
2–3 garlic cloves, crushed
1 tbsp vegetable oil
55g button or chestnut mushrooms, sliced
300g red kidney beans, either cooked from dry (see Red Kidney Beans on page 138) or tinned, drained
400g tin of tomatoes
2 tsp Marmite or Vegemite
pinch of cayenne pepper
1–2 tbsp tomato purée
1 tsp soft light brown sugar
sea salt and freshly ground black pepper

Method
1. Sauté the onions, pepper and garlic in the oil for 10–15 minutes until soft. Add the mushrooms, cooked beans and tinned tomatoes and stir.
2. Add the Marmite or Vegemite, cayenne pepper, tomato purée, brown sugar, salt and pepper and mix well. Cover and allow to simmer for a further 15–20 minutes. Serve.

Red Split Lentil and Cheese Loaf

Feeds 4. Serve with Jacket Potatoes (see page 133) and salad

You will need a pyrex or ceramic baking dish, about 22 x 17cm

2 carrots, grated
2 onions, sliced
1–2 garlic cloves, crushed and chopped
1–2 tbsp vegetable oil
115g sage and onion stuffing (dry)
170g red split lentils, cooked for use in flans and loaves
    (see Red Split Lentils on page 140), drained
1 tbsp tomato purée
30g breadcrumbs
115g cheese, grated (mozzarella, strong Cheddar or Gouda all work
    and produce slightly different results in flavour and texture)
2 eggs
sea salt and freshly ground black pepper

Method

1. Preheat the oven to 190°C (375°F), Gas 5. Sauté the vegetables in oil for approximately 15 minutes in a large frying pan then remove from the heat.
2. Add the stuffing to the cooked, drained lentils in the saucepan and mix together, then add the mixture to the vegetables in the frying pan. If the mixture is looking a little dry, added a little boiling water to the mix.
3. Season with salt and pepper and add the tomato purée and breadcrumbs. Allow to cool. Once cool, add the cheese, crack in the eggs and mix well.
4. Spoon the mixture into your baking dish and bake in the oven for 20 minutes.

Spinach Pasties with Cream Cheese and Mash

Makes 6

340g unfilled pasty circles (follow steps 1–2 of the Crumbly Pastry: Pasties recipe on page 128)

Filling
170g spinach
1 small onion, chopped
knob of butter
3 potatoes (weighing approximately 650–700g uncooked), mashed (for a reminder of how to make mashed potato, see Buttery Mash on page 135 but don't add butter or seasoning)
285g cream cheese
1 tbsp chopped chives
sea salt and freshly ground black pepper

Method
1. Preheat the oven to 180°C (350°F), Gas 4. Cut off any thick stalks from the spinach, then shred the leaves. Over a medium heat, sauté the onion in a small knob of butter for 5 minutes or until softened. Add the spinach and sauté for 1–2 minutes, stirring once or twice, until completely wilted.
2. In a large bowl, combine the mashed potatoes and cream cheese, then add the onion and spinach mix and the chives. Season to taste with salt and pepper.
2. Follow steps 3–5 of the Crumbly Pastry: Pasties recipe (see page 128), baking the pasties in the oven for 25–30 minutes or until golden brown and the pastry is crisp.

Red Pepper Risotto

Feeds 4

3 carrots, grated
3 onions, sliced
1–2 garlic cloves, crushed
115g peas (fresh or frozen)
1–2 tbsp sunflower oil
1 tsp ground turmeric
250ml stock (boiled water mixed with 1 tsp Marmite or Vegemite)
340g cooked Brown Rice (see page 137)
1 red pepper, deseeded and sliced
sea salt and freshly ground black pepper

Method

1. Sauté the carrots, onions, garlic, most of the red pepper and peas in the oil in a large frying pan for 10 minutes. Add the turmeric and stock, cover and simmer gently for 5–10 minutes.
2. Add the cooked rice and simmer gently, uncovered, for a further 10–15 minutes, stirring occasionally. Season to taste with salt and pepper. Scatter over the remaining slices of red pepper and combine. Serve immediately.

Tofu Stir-Fry with Broccoli, Carrot and Ginger

Feeds 4. Serve with rice or noodles, and salad

2 tbsp plain white flour
250g pack of firm tofu, drained and cubed
1 tbsp vegetable oil
2 carrots, sliced diagonally
1 onion, sliced
1 small head of broccoli, chopped into florets
1 red pepper, deseeded and diced
1 small piece of fresh root ginger, grated
pinch of chilli flakes
1 tbsp soy sauce
1 tbsp soft light brown sugar
sea salt and freshly ground black pepper

Method

1. Place the flour in a small plastic bag and season with salt and pepper. Put the tofu cubes in the bag and shake until they become coated with the flour and seasoning.
2. Heat the oil in a frying pan until very hot, then add the tofu and stir-fry until golden brown on all sides. Remove the tofu from the pan and set aside.
3. Sauté the carrots and onion in the frying pan for 10 minutes, then add the broccoli, pepper and ginger and sauté for another 5–10 minutes.
4. Season the vegetables with salt, the chilli flakes, soy sauce and sugar and stir. Add the tofu and stir-fry for 5 minutes until heated through.

– ALTERNATIVELY –

° Try other vegetables like mushrooms, pak choi, sweetcorn, peas, green beans, cauliflower, spring onions, sweet potatoes or garlic.

Sautéed Vegetables

Virtually any combination of vegetables can be sautéed, but less dense vegetables like mushrooms, sweetcorn, peas and peppers are better suited to it.

Feeds 4 as part of a main meal served with rice or pasta

2–3 tbsp sunflower oil
3 carrots, sliced diagonally
1 onion, sliced
1 red pepper, deseeded and sliced
225g courgettes, sliced lengthways
115g peas (fresh or frozen)
225g beansprouts
1–2 tbsp soy sauce
sea salt and freshly ground black pepper

Method

1. Heat the oil in a large frying pan and when hot, add the carrots. Stir, cover and sauté gently for 5 minutes, giving the pan a shake every so often to ensure the carrot cooks evenly.
2. Add the rest of the vegetables apart from the beansprouts and sauté, covered, for a further 5 minutes, shaking the pan as before, then add the beansprouts.
3. Stir well, season with salt and pepper and add the soy sauce. Cover and simmer gently for another 5 minutes, stirring often. Serve.

FISH AND SEAFOOD

Mackerel in Zesty Lemon Sauce

Makes 2. Feeds 4 as part of a main dish with Brown Rice (see page 137)

2 tbsp lemon juice
1 tsp runny honey
1 carrot, thinly sliced
1 onion, thinly sliced
2 fresh mackerel, gutted, cleaned and filleted (ask your fishmonger to prepare the fish for you, then remove the skin after cooking if desired)
30g butter or margarine
30g plain white flour
1 tsp curry powder
flat-leaf parsley, finely chopped, for sprinkling
sea salt and freshly ground black pepper

Method

1. Add the lemon juice, honey, carrot, onion and 300ml of water to a large saucepan, season with salt and pepper and slowly bring to the boil, then reduce the heat and simmer gently for 5 minutes.
2. Add the mackerel, cover and cook gently for 5 minutes until tender. Remove from the heat, then remove the fish from the saucepan and keep warm by wrapping in foil. Strain 100ml of the stock in the saucepan and set aside, leaving the remaining stock in the pan.
3. Melt the butter or margarine in a small saucepan, stir in the flour and cook for 1 minute over a low heat. Slowly add the strained fish stock and the curry powder and stir until smooth and creamy.
4. Return the fish to the main saucepan containing the stock and add the sauce. Bring to the boil, then reduce the heat and simmer gently for 5 minutes. Sprinkle with the parsley before serving.

....

Crispy Fish Fillets

Feeds 4. Perfect with Chunky Oven Chips (see page 136) and salad

4 small skinless, boneless fillets of white fish such as haddock, cod or sea bass (if using fresh fish ask your fishmonger to clean, fillet and debone the fish)

Crispy Coating
70g fine polenta
1 tbsp plain white flour
1 tsp turmeric
pinch of chilli powder or dried chilli flakes
2 egg whites, beaten for 1 minute and transferred to a shallow bowl
1 tbsp vegetable oil

Method
1. Mix together the dry ingredients for the crispy coating in a shallow bowl.
2. Dip each fish fillet first in the polenta mixture, then in the beaten egg white and then again in the polenta mixture.
3. Place the coated fillets on a plate, cover and refrigerate for 10–15 minutes.
4. Heat the oil in a large cast-iron frying pan and fry the fillets for 3 minutes on each side until golden. Serve.

Layered Fish Bake with a Crunchy Parmesan Topping

Feeds 4. Serve with peas and roasted carrots, or any sautéed vegetables in season

You will need an oblong pie dish approximately 23 x 19cm

680g skinless white fish, filleted and deboned
1 tbsp vegetable oil
2 tsp chopped flat-leaf parsley
1 onion, grated or finely chopped
2 eggs
570ml milk
sea salt and freshly ground black pepper

Topping
2 tbsp breadcrumbs
55g butter or margarine
55g Gruyère or Parmesan cheese, grated

Method

1. Preheat the oven to 180°C (350°F), Gas 4. Grease the pie dish, then briefly sauté the fish in the oil for 3–5 minutes. Allow the fish to cool then flake the meat.
2. Layer the fish, parsley and onion in the prepared pie dish, starting with the fish.
3. Beat the eggs with a fork and gradually add the milk. Season with salt and pepper and pour the mixture over the fish.
4. Bake in the oven for 25 minutes, or until the top feels firm.
5. Top with a mixture of the breadcrumbs, the butter or margarine and the grated cheese, then pop under the grill for 3–4 minutes until the cheese is golden brown.

Traditional Fish and Sweetcorn Pie

Feeds 4. Serve with steamed greens

You will need an overproof pie dish approximately 23 x 19cm

455g boneless and skinless fish, cooked and flaked (try half smoked haddock and half frozen cod, salmon or plaice cooked according to pack instructions. If using fresh fish ask your fishmonger to clean, fillet and debone the fish, then remove the skin after cooking)
115g sweetcorn (tinned, fresh or frozen)
300ml Basic Béchamel Sauce (see page 146)
900g mashed potato (see Buttery Mash on page 135)
sea salt and freshly ground black pepper

Method

1. Preheat the oven to 180°C (350°F), Gas 4. Make an even layer of the flaked fish and sweetcorn in the pie dish, season with salt and pepper and pour over the béchamel sauce.
2. Top with the mashed potato and bake in the oven for 15 minutes or until golden brown.

– ALTERNATIVELY –

° Use mushrooms or other vegetables when sweetcorn is not available.

Mushroom-Stuffed Mackerel

*Feeds 4 as part of a main dish with Jacket Potatoes
(see page 133) and salad*

knob of butter
115g button mushrooms, sliced or halved
2 tsp oatmeal
2 large fresh mackerel, gutted and cleaned but left whole (ask your fishmonger to prepare the fish for you, then remove the skin after cooking if desired)
2 tbsp vegetable oil
sea salt and freshly ground black pepper

Method

1. Grease an ovenproof dish, and preheat the oven to 180°C (350°F), Gas 4. Melt a knob of butter in a large frying pan, add the mushrooms and sauté for 3–4 minutes or until golden brown. Add the oatmeal, season with salt and pepper and combine.
2. Use this mixture to stuff the belly cavity of the mackerel.
3. Brush the mackerel with the oil and place them side by side in the prepared ovenproof dish and bake for approximately 25 minutes or until the flesh flakes easily away from the bone.

Crunchy Oat-Coated Herring
Feeds 4 as part of a main meal

4 fresh herring fillets
1–2 eggs, beaten and transferred to a shallow dish
2 tbsp fine oatmeal, in a shallow dish
1–2 tbsp sunflower oil
sea salt and freshly ground black pepper

Method
Dip the herring fillets in the beaten egg, then roll in the oatmeal and
shallow fry in oil until brown on both sides. Season with salt and
pepper before serving.

....

Fragrant Coconut Fish
Feeds 4. Serve over Brown Rice (see page 137) with salad

450g skinless boneless fish fillets – cod, halibut or snapper are good
     (if using fresh fish, ask your fishmonger to clean, fillet and
     debone the fish, then remove the skin after cooking)
1 tbsp vegetable oil
55g butter or margarine
2 onions, finely chopped
1 apple, peeled and finely chopped
2 tbsp plain white flour
1 tsp Marmite or Vegemite
1 tsp curry powder
100ml cream or natural yoghurt
1 tbsp lemon juice
30g desiccated coconut
sea salt and freshly ground black pepper

Method

1. Lightly sauté the fish in the oil for 5–10 minutes in a large covered pan until just tender, then remove from the pan. Melt the butter in the pan and fry the onions and apple for 3–5 minutes until soft.
2. Stir in the flour and gradually add 285ml of water. Add the Marmite or Vegemite and curry powder and simmer gently over a low heat for 5 minutes.
3. Add the cream or yoghurt, lemon juice and coconut and continue to simmer for 5–10 minutes.
4. Return the fish to the pan and marinate for a further 5–10 minutes over a low heat. When the fish is firm and opaque, it is ready. Pour the sauce over the fish and season with salt and pepper to serve.

....

Homemade Fishcakes

Feeds 8–12. Serve with steamed cauliflower and salad

900g mashed potato (see Buttery Mash on page 135)
455g skinless, boneless cod or haddock fillets, simmered in 300ml of half milk, half water for 5–10 minutes, then flaked
1 tsp tomato purée
1 tsp Marmite or Vegemite
2 slices of wholemeal bread, grated to make breadcrumbs
1 egg, beaten
plain white flour, for shaping
2–3 tbsp vegetable oil
sea salt and freshly ground black pepper

Method

1. Mix together the mashed potatoes, fish, tomato purée and Marmite or Vegemite. Add the breadcrumbs to the mixture along with the beaten egg, season with salt and pepper and mix well.

2. Form into small cakes and roll them in a little flour. Fry the
   fishcakes on both sides in the oil until brown or bake for
   10–15 minutes in a preheated oven at 200°C (400°F), Gas 6.

....

Spicy Battered Mackerel

Feeds 4. Serve with buttery Jacket Potatoes (see page 133), peas and salad

3 small fresh mackerel, gutted, cleaned and filleted (ask your
   fishmonger to prepare the fish for you, then remove the skin after
   cooking if desired)

Batter
225g self-raising wholemeal flour
1 tsp salt
pinch of cayenne pepper
1 egg, beaten
250ml milk
6 tbsp vegetable oil

Method
1. Mix together the flour, salt and cayenne pepper, then add the egg
   and combine. Gradually stir in the milk to form a batter.
2. Heat the oil in a frying pan until sizzling. Coat the mackerel in
   the batter and fry in the hot oil for approximately 5 minutes on
   each side until golden brown.
3. Keep the fish warm in the oven until ready to serve.

Sweet Potato, Coriander and Chilli Fishcakes

Feeds 4

900g sweet potatoes, scrubbed or peeled and diced
good pinch of chilli powder
2 tsp corn oil
bunch of coriander leaves, finely chopped
450g skinless, boneless cod or haddock fillets, simmered in 300ml
     of half milk, half water for 5–10 minutes, then flaked
1 egg, beaten
2 slices of wholemeal bread, grated to form breadcrumbs
30ml corn oil, for frying
sea salt and freshly ground black pepper

Method

1. In a large saucepan, boil the sweet potatoes in salted water for 12–15 minutes until just tender. Do not let them become mushy as a nice firm texture is needed to form the cakes.
2. Drain the sweet potatoes and season them with salt and pepper, the chilli powder, the corn oil and the coriander. Mash well.
3. Mix the fish and mashed sweet potato mixture together and form into 8–12 patty cakes. Dip the cakes in the beaten egg and coat in the breadcrumbs. Fry in corn oil for about 10 minutes, turning once, until golden.

Baked Mackerel with Lemon and Mustard

Feeds 4 as part of a main meal

You will need a large ovenproof dish

30g butter or margarine
1 small onion, finely chopped
85g wholemeal breadcrumbs
grated zest and juice of 1 small lemon
1 tbsp mustard (wholegrain is best here)
1 egg yolk
4 small fresh mackerel, gutted, cleaned and deboned (ask your
  fishmonger to prepare the fish for you)
2 tsp plain white flour
handful of coriander leaves, chopped, for sprinkling
sea salt and freshly ground black pepper

Method

1. Grease your ovenproof dish and preheat the oven to 180°C
   (350°F), Gas 4. Heat half the butter or margarine in a frying pan,
   add the onion and fry until soft. Remove from the heat and stir
   in the breadcrumbs, grated lemon zest, mustard and egg yolk,
   and then season with salt and pepper.
2. Press approximately 2 tablespoons of the mixture into the belly
   cavity of each fish. Lie the mackerel in the dish and make deep
   slashes across each fish.
3. Dust the fish lightly with the flour. Pour over the lemon juice
   and dot with the remaining butter or margarine. Bake uncovered
   for about 20–30 minutes in the oven, basting frequently.
4. Crisp the skin a little more under a hot grill if desired. Sprinkle
   with the chopped coriander before serving.

Spicy Prawn Rice with Fried Tomatoes

Feeds 4

1 head of garlic, segmented and crushed
1 onion, sliced
2 tbsp olive oil
200g fresh raw prawns, peeled, washed and veins removed
6 tomatoes, chopped
1 tbsp soy sauce
1–2 pinches of chilli powder or chilli flakes
680g cooked Brown Rice (see page 137)
sea salt and freshly ground black pepper

Method

1. Gently fry the garlic and onion in the oil for 5 minutes over a low heat. Cover and allow to cook for a further 10 minutes, stirring occasionally.
2. Increase the heat slightly, then add the prawns, tomatoes, soy sauce and chilli and stir-fry for 5 minutes.
3. Add the cooked rice and stir. Cover and allow to cook over a low-medium heat for 15–20 minutes, stirring regularly.
4. Season with salt and pepper and serve.

Chilli Prawns in Coconut Cream

Feeds 4. Serve with rice or noodles

1–2 tbsp vegetable oil
1 onion, thinly sliced
1–2 garlic cloves (to taste), crushed
1 small piece of fresh root ginger, crushed
2 red or green chillies, finely chopped
1 tsp turmeric
1 tbsp finely chopped coriander leaves (fresh or dried)
200g prawns (fresh or frozen), peeled and veins removed
100g creamed coconut, crumbled
juice of 1 lemon or lime
sea salt and freshly ground black pepper

Method

1. Heat the oil in a frying pan over a medium heat. Add the onion, garlic and ginger and stir-fry for 5 minutes.
2. Then add the chopped chillies, turmeric, coriander and a pinch of sea salt to taste, then stir-fry for 3 minutes. Toss in the prawns and stir-fry for another 5 minutes.
3. Crumble in the coconut and, stirring constantly, gradually add 250ml of boiling water, until the sauce becomes a thick gravy that coats the prawns. Simmer gently for 5 minutes, while continuing to stir regularly.
4. Sprinkle with the lemon or lime juice and season to taste with salt and pepper, then serve.

Fish and Vegetable Stir-Fry with Dry Cider

Feeds 4

4 small skinless, boneless white fish fillets, fresh or frozen (cod, haddock or red snapper work well. If using fresh fish, ask your fishmonger to clean, fillet and debone the fish, then remove the skin after cooking)

1–2 tbsp olive oil

1 onion, finely sliced

1–3 garlic cloves (to taste), crushed

1 small head of broccoli, chopped into florets

1 red pepper, deseeded and sliced

90g frozen mixed vegetables

pinch of chilli flakes

1 tsp turmeric

1 tbsp soy sauce

290ml dry sparkling cider

170g long grain rice, cooked according to pack instructions

sea salt and freshly ground black pepper

Method

1. Lightly sauté the fish in half the olive oil, turning regularly, for 5 minutes until the fish is just starting to flake. Remove the fish from the pan and set aside in a covered dish.

2. Add the rest of the olive oil to the pan and sauté the onion, garlic, broccoli and pepper for 5 minutes, then add the frozen vegetables. Stir and season with the chilli flakes, turmeric, soy sauce, and salt and pepper to taste.

3. Gradually add the cider, stirring constantly, then stir in the cooked rice. Stir-fry for 10–15 minutes, then add the fish and stir gently for 5–10 minutes, until the fish flakes into the rice and vegetables. Serve immediately.

MEAT AND POULTRY

Honey-Roast Chicken

Feeds 4, with enough left over for lunch the next day. Keep hold of the roast chicken carcass and bones to make homemade stock (see page 39).

You will need a roasting tin approximately 35 x 30cm

1 small roasting chicken without giblets (approximately 1.3kg)*
85g sage and onion stuffing, prepared according to packet instructions
1–2 tbsp vegetable oil

Honey Baste
1 tsp salt
1–2 tsp soy sauce
2 tsp runny honey
pinch of cayenne pepper
2 tsp vegetable oil

* Adjust cooking times according to the weight of your chicken after stuffing – as a general rule you should allow 20 minutes per 500g plus an extra 20 minutes cooking time

Method

1. Preheat the oven to 200°C (400°F), Gas 6. Place the chicken in the roasting tin. Remove any visible fat from the body cavity and fill with the sage and onion stuffing.
2. Brush with a little oil and roast for 45 minutes. Remove from the oven and brush with the honey baste. Reduce the oven temperature to 190°C (375°F), Gas 5. Roast the chicken for a further 30–45 minutes until the juices run clear when the chicken thigh is pierced with a skewer, the skin is brown and crispy, the meat is tender and the stuffing is piping hot throughout.
3. Allow to rest for at least 10 minutes before carving. Serve with the pan juices.

....

Caribbean Spiced Lamb Shanks

Feeds 4. Sweet Potato Mash (see page 136) makes a good accompaniment

You will need either a slow cooker or a large lidded saucepan

1 tbsp vegetable oil
2 lamb shanks (approximately 500g each)
2 large onions, chopped
6 garlic cloves, crushed

Caribbean Sauce

1 tsp chilli powder
1 tsp ground ginger

1 tsp mixed spice
1 tsp garlic powder
1 tsp sea salt
1 tsp soft light brown sugar
1 tbsp tomato purée
4 tbsp plain yoghurt

Method

1. Heat the oil in a large frying pan and brown the lamb on all sides with the onions and garlic for 2–3 minutes, stirring often.
2. Make the Caribbean sauce by mixing all the ingredients together with 300ml of boiled water that has slightly cooled.
3. Place the lamb shanks, onions and garlic in a slow cooker and pour over the Caribbean sauce, then allow to cook for 6–8 hours on a low setting. Alternatively, simmer the lamb shanks, onions, garlic and Caribbean sauce together over a low heat for 3 hours in a large, covered saucepan until the meat has fallen away from the bone.

Slow-Roast Shoulder of Pork with Apple

Feeds 4. Delicious surrounded by the apples and roast vegetables. Make gravy from the roast juices and serve with green vegetables

You will need a deep roasting tin approximately 35 x 30cm

1 tbsp sunflower oil
half a shoulder of pork (approximately 1.5kg)
3 garlic cloves, thinly sliced
600g potatoes, scrubbed or peeled and chopped into large pieces
    (Desirée, Romano, Maris Piper or King Edward varieties are
    best for roasting)

2 carrots, chopped into large chunks
2 apples, quartered
1 tsp sea salt
sprinkle of chilli powder or dried chilli flakes

Method

1. Preheat the oven to 220°C (425°F), Gas 7. Drizzle the oil in the roasting tin and roll the joint in the oil. With a sharp knife make tiny slits all over the pork and insert the garlic slices.
2. Roast the pork in the oven for 10–15 minutes.
3. Remove the tin from the oven and reduce the temperature to 170°C (325°F), Gas 3. Add the potatoes, carrots and apples to the tin and stir them in the roasting juices.
4. Cover the tin with foil and roast for 45–60 minutes at the lower temperature, basting occasionally.
5. Remove from the oven. Sprinkle over the salt and chilli and baste.
6. Return to the oven and cook uncovered for 15–30 minutes until tender and succulent.

Gravy
Makes 300ml

Method

1. Pour away most of the fat from the roasting tin, draining it from one corner, and leave the sediment behind.
2. Season with salt and pepper, stir in 1 tablespoon of plain white flour, blend well, transfer to a saucepan and cook over a low heat until the mixture turns brown.
3. Slowly stir in 300ml of hot water from the kettle and simmer for 2–3 minutes until the gravy reaches pouring consistency.

Slow Beef and Onion Stew

Feeds 4

You will need either a slow cooker or a large lidded frying pan

2 tbsp vegetable oil
500g chopped stewing steak
2 tbsp plain white flour
4 onions, roughly chopped
2 carrots, chopped into large chunks
1 parsnip, chopped into large chunks

Stock
1 tsp Marmite or Vegemite
1 tbsp tomato purée
1 tsp balsamic vinegar
1 tbsp red wine vinegar
sea salt and freshly ground black pepper

Method
1. Heat the oil in a large frying pan and brown the beef on all sides for 2–3 minutes.
2. Remove the meat, sprinkle the flour into the remaining fat in the frying pan and stir well.
3. Mix together the stock ingredients with 300ml of boiled water and add to the frying pan with the flour and fat. Simmer and stir for 2 minutes.
4. Either put the beef and vegetables in the slow cooker with the stock from the pan poured over and cook for 8–9 hours on a low setting or cook the steak, vegetables and stock over the lowest heat in the pan, covered, for 6–8 hours, stirring occasionally.

Kidney and Bacon Pilaff

Feeds 4

1–2 tbsp vegetable oil
115g streaky bacon, chopped
340g lamb's kidneys, washed, skinned, halved and cored, and
     cut into bite-size pieces
1 large onion, sliced
115g chestnut or button mushrooms, sliced
285–500ml stock (boiled water mixed with 1 tsp Marmite or Vegemite)
1 tbsp plain wholemeal flour
340g cooked Brown Rice (see page 137)
sea salt and freshly ground black pepper

Method

1. Heat the oil in a frying pan then fry the bacon for 2–3 minutes.
   Add the kidneys, season well with salt and pepper and fry for
   5–10 minutes, turning occasionally. Add the onion, reduce to
   a low heat and cover. Sauté for a further 5 minutes.

2. Add the mushrooms and sauté for 2–3 minutes over a medium
   heat. Then stir in 285ml of the stock, cover and reduce to a low
   heat. Simmer until everything is tender, which should take about
   20–30 minutes, stirring frequently. Add more stock as needed if
   the mixture is looking a little dry.

3. Sprinkle in the flour and stir constantly over a medium heat until
   the sauce thickens – about 2–3 minutes. Combine the kidneys,
   bacon and sauce with the cooked brown rice and serve. Scatter
   over a little chopped flat-leaf parsley before serving if you have
   any to hand to give the dish a little colour.

Mama's Pan Chicken

Feeds 4. Serve with rice and peas

1 small chicken, divided into 8 pieces (ask your butcher to do
  this if necessary)
1 onion, sliced
2–3 garlic cloves (to taste), crushed
1 red chilli, sliced
3–4 cloves
1 bay leaf
280ml Guinness
280ml dark malt vinegar
2 tsp salt
sea salt and freshly ground black pepper

Method

1. Place the chicken in a large lidded pan, pot or dish along with the
   onion, garlic, chilli, cloves and bay leaf.
2. Pour over the Guinness and vinegar, sprinkle over the 2 teaspoons
   of salt and stir. Cover and leave overnight at room temperature.
3. Stir the chicken and bring the pan to the boil. Boil vigorously for
   10 minutes, then reduce the heat, cover and simmer very gently for
   2 hours, stirring and basting occasionally. If the chicken looks a
   little dry during cooking, pour over some water. Season to taste with
   salt and pepper. Serve the chicken in its sauce with rice and peas.

Note on chicken

Make sure that any uncooked chicken is well wrapped when stored
in the refrigerator and not in direct contact with any other food.
Take care to ensure that any worktops used to prepare raw chicken
are washed down thoroughly afterwards.

Lemon Honey Lamb Shoulder with Potatoes and Fresh Thyme

Feeds 4

You will need either a slow cooker or a lidded casserole dish

2 tbsp sunflower oil
700g shoulder of lamb or leg steaks (get your butcher to cut
    the shoulder into 4 large chunks through the bone)
2 onions, chopped
2–3 garlic cloves, crushed
1 tbsp thyme leaves
1 tsp grated lemon zest
500g potatoes, scrubbed or peeled and thinly sliced or diced into
    1cm chunks (Desirée, Romano, Maris Piper or King Edward
    varieties produce the best roast potatoes but you can use any)

Lemon Stock
200ml lemon juice
100ml sour cream
2 tsp runny honey
1 tsp soy sauce
2 tsp salt
1 tsp turmeric
freshly ground black pepper

Method
1. In a large frying pan, heat the oil over a medium-high heat. Brown the lamb on all sides with the onions, garlic, thyme and lemon zest for 2–3 minutes.
2. Add the potatoes and stir-fry for a further 2–3 minutes. Remove from the heat and then mix the lemon stock ingredients together.

3. Place the lamb and vegetables in a slow cooker, cover with the lemon stock and cook on a low setting for 8 hours. Alternatively, slow roast everything in a covered casserole dish for 4–6 hours at 150°C (300°F), Gas 2. If oven-cooking, check the lamb and liquid level halfway through cooking and add water if the mixture is looking a little dry.

– ALTERNATIVELY –

◦ Cook the potatoes separately (see New Potatoes on page 134, but exclude the dill).

Sticky Spare Rib Chops
Feeds 4 as part of a main meal

You will need a large ovenproof casserole dish

680g spare rib pork chops about 1cm thick
1 tbsp plain wholemeal flour

Sauce
2 tsp salt
1 tbsp sugar
1 tbsp red wine vinegar
1 tbsp soy sauce
150ml apple juice
pinch of cayenne pepper

Method
1. Mix the sauce ingredients together in a heavy-based saucepan or casserole dish. Add 300ml of cold water and stir.
2. Add the chops to the sauce. Bring to the boil, cover and simmer

gently for about 45–60 minutes, turning the chops occasionally.
3. When the meat is tender, sprinkle the flour into the sauce, stirring
   continually until the sauce thickens. Serve with the sauce poured
   over the chops.

....

Creole Corn-Crust Chicken

Feeds 4 as part of a main meal

115g plain wholemeal flour
400ml buttermilk
1 tsp hot pepper sauce
4 small chicken breasts
3–4 tbsp vegetable oil, for shallow frying
sea salt

Corn Coating
60g plain wholemeal flour
140g fine polenta
1 tsp garlic powder
1 tsp onion powder
1 tsp chilli powder
1 tsp turmeric
1 tsp cumin powder
pinch of salt

Method
1. Preheat the oven to 190°C (375°F), Gas 5. Mix together the
   ingredients for the corn coating and transfer to a shallow dish.
2. Place the wholemeal flour in a separate shallow dish. Pour
   the buttermilk into another shallow dish and stir in the hot
   pepper sauce.

3. Lightly season the chicken breasts with salt and dip each one first into the flour, then the spicy buttermilk and lastly, the corn coating.
4. Keep the chicken breasts on a sheet of greaseproof paper until ready to fry.
5. Heat 1–2 tablespoons of the oil in a large cast-iron pan and fry each chicken breast for 4 minutes on each side over a medium heat until golden and crispy.
6. Bake for a further 5 minutes in the oven for a crispier crust.

....

Chicken Macaroni
Feeds 4

225g wholewheat macaroni
1 chicken piece, roasted (a leg or thigh is ideal)
115g frozen peas
2–3 garlic cloves (to taste), crushed
2 onions, sliced
2 carrots, grated
2–3 tbsp vegetable oil
1 tbsp soy sauce
400g tin of chopped tomatoes
pinch of cayenne pepper
1 tbsp tomato purée
sea salt and freshly ground black pepper

Method
1. In a large saucepan, bring 1.75 litres of salted water to the boil and add the macaroni. Stir, cover and simmer for 10–12 minutes until almost soft. Drain and set aside.
2. Cut the cooked chicken into bite-size pieces. Sauté the peas, garlic, onions and carrots in the oil for about 10 minutes, then add the

soy sauce, the chicken and the chopped tomatoes. Season with
cayenne pepper and salt and pepper and stir in the tomato purée.
3. Simmer over a low heat for 1–2 minutes. Add the macaroni, stir
and simmer for a further 5–10 minutes, then serve.

....

Pork and Beans

Feeds 4. Serve with mashed potatoes or brown rice and salad
(see Buttery Mash on page 135 and Brown Rice on page 137)

You will need a deep ovenproof casserole dish

680g spare rib pork chops
1 tbsp vegetable oil
1 large onion, sliced
2–3 garlic cloves (to taste), crushed
130g black-eyed beans, either cooked from dry (see Black-Eyed
    Beans on page 139; the simmering time can be decreased to
    25 minutes as there are fewer beans) or tinned, with their water
400g tin of chopped tomatoes
2 tbsp soy sauce
1 tsp soft light brown sugar
1 tsp balsamic vinegar
sea salt and freshly ground black pepper

Method
1. Preheat the oven to 190°C (375°F), Gas 5.
2. Fry the chops lightly in the oil for 3 minutes on each side
   until brown.
3. Add the onion and garlic to the pork and fry for 5 minutes until
   the onions are soft and golden.
4. Add the beans with their water, the chopped tomatoes and the soy

sauce, season with salt and pepper then add the brown sugar and balsamic vinegar. Simmer for a further 5 minutes, then turn the mixture into a deep ovenproof casserole dish.
5. Cover with foil and bake for 45–60 minutes.

....

Chicken and Mushroom Casserole

Feeds 4. Serve with Butter Dumplings (see page 130)

You will need an ovenproof casserole dish

2 tbsp vegetable oil
4 skinless chicken joints (as the breast or thigh parts have the
   most meat on them they are generally preferred, but any joint
   can be used)
plain white flour, for coating
500g potatoes, scrubbed or peeled and diced
2 carrots, chopped
2 onions, sliced
2–4 garlic cloves (to taste), crushed
60g button or chestnut mushrooms, sliced
60g peas (fresh or frozen)
500ml stock (boiled water mixed with 3 tsp Marmite or Vegemite)
2 tsp white wine vinegar
1 tbsp tomato purée
sea salt and freshly ground black pepper

Method
1. Preheat the oven to 190°C (375°F), Gas 5. Heat the oil in a large pan over a medium heat, then coat the chicken joints with flour seasoned with salt and pepper and brown on all sides in the vegetable oil. The sautéeing time will vary depending on the size and

shape of the joints used, but between 10–15 minutes is a good guide.
2. Place the chicken joints in an ovenproof casserole dish with all the vegetables.
3. Mix the stock and vinegar with the tomato purée and pour over the chicken and vegetables. Place in the oven for 1 hour and serve immediately.

....

Ham and Mushroom Wholewheat Spaghetti in Tomato Sauce
Feeds 4

340g wholewheat spaghetti
170g cooked shoulder ham, whole
115g chestnut or button mushrooms, sliced
1 tbsp olive oil

Tomato Sauce
3 onions, sliced
3 celery sticks, chopped
1 tbsp olive oil
400g tin of chopped tomatoes
1 tsp soft light brown sugar
2 tsp soy sauce
pinch of chilli powder or dried chilli flakes
sea salt and freshly ground black pepper

Method
1. First, make the tomato sauce. Sauté the onions and celery in the olive oil for 10 minutes, then transfer to a saucepan with the chopped tomatoes.
2. Add the brown sugar and soy sauce, then season with the salt,

pepper and chilli. On the lowest heat, bring to a gentle simmer, stirring regularly.

3. Meanwhile, bring a large pan of salted water to the boil and add the spaghetti. Boil until the spaghetti becomes quite tender, which should take approximately 10 minutes, then drain.

4. Cut the ham into strips and sauté lightly in a large pan with the mushrooms in olive oil for 3–5 minutes. Drain and fold in the cooked spaghetti and toss until well glazed.

5. Serve with the tomato sauce and a simple salad.

....

Chicken-Fried Rice

Feeds 4

1–2 tbsp vegetable oil
2 chicken pieces (breast is quickest and easiest as there is
   no need to debone)
115g white cabbage, finely shredded
2 onions, sliced
115g peas (fresh or frozen)
340g of cooked Brown Rice (see page 137)
1–2 tbsp soy sauce
2–3 tbsp grapefruit juice
pinch of chilli powder or dried chilli flakes
1 tsp paprika
1 tsp balsamic vinegar
sea salt and freshly ground black pepper

Method

1. Heat the oil in a large frying pan. Sauté the chicken pieces for about 20 minutes until cooked through.

2. Remove the chicken from the pan, debone if necessary and shred.

3. Sauté the cabbage and onion in the pan for 10 minutes over a

medium heat. Add the peas and sauté for a further 5 minutes.

4. Add the rice and stir until combined.

5. Add the chicken, soy sauce, grapefruit juice, chilli, paprika and balsamic vinegar. Season with salt and pepper and stir-fry for a further 5–10 minutes. Serve.

....

Rich Chicken and Mixed Vegetable Curry

Feeds 4. Serve over Brown Rice (see page 137).
Great for using up leftover roast chicken

2 tbsp vegetable oil
2 celery sticks, chopped
3 onions, sliced
2–4 garlic cloves (to taste), crushed
1 green pepper, deseeded and sliced
55g button or chestnut mushrooms, sliced
5 tsp curry powder
400g tin of chopped tomatoes
2 chicken leg or breast quarters, cut into bite-size pieces
2 tbsp soy sauce
1 tbsp tomato purée
sea salt and freshly ground black pepper

Method

1. Heat the oil in a large frying pan and sauté the vegetables for about 10 minutes. Add the curry powder, fry for a minute or so, then add the chopped tomatoes and chicken pieces and stir.

2. Add the soy sauce and simmer gently for 15 minutes, stirring occasionally.

3. Add the tomato purée, season with salt and pepper and simmer for a further 10 minutes. Serve.

Slow Lamb Hot Pot

Feeds 4

You will need either a slow cooker, a large lidded casserole dish or a large lidded saucepan

2 tbsp vegetable oil
4 lamb neck fillets (approximately 700g in total)
1 large onion, chopped
1 leek, chopped
2 carrots, chopped
500g potatoes, scrubbed or peeled and thickly sliced
flat-leaf parsley, chopped, for sprinkling

Stock
1 tsp soy sauce
1 tsp Marmite or Vegemite
1 tbsp red wine vinegar
1 tsp balsamic vinegar
pinch of chilli powder or dried chilli flakes
sea salt and freshly ground black pepper

Method
Heat the oil in a frying pan and brown the lamb fillets for 2–3 minutes on all sides.

Option 1
1. Place the onion, leek and carrots in the slow cooker, add the lamb fillets and top with a layer of potato slices.
2. Mix together the stock ingredients with 300ml of boiled water and pour over the lamb fillets and vegetables.
3. Cover and cook on a low setting for 6–8 hours until the meat is tender.

Option 2

Mix together the stock ingredients with 300ml of boiled water and pour over the lamb fillets and vegetables in the casserole dish. Roast for 3–4 hours on 150°C (300°F), Gas 2.

Option 3

Mix together the stock ingredients with 300ml of boiled water and simmer the lamb fillets and vegetables in the stock over the lowest heat in a large, covered saucepan for 3–4 hours. Serve sprinkled with chopped flat-leaf parsley.

....

Chicken and Sweetcorn Pie

Feeds 4–6. Great for using up leftover chicken from a roast

1 Crumbly Pastry case, blind baked and lining a 24cm round pie dish, 5cm deep, with a third of the pastry left over for the lid (see steps 1–2 of Crumbly Pastry, page 127)

Filling

300–350g chicken (leg or breast quarter)
2 tbsp olive oil
4 small onions, sliced
1 tbsp vegetable oil
100g sweetcorn (tinned, fresh or frozen)
100g spinach, shredded
600ml Basic Béchamel Sauce (see page 146)
milk, for glazing
sea salt and freshly ground black pepper

Method

1. Preheat the oven to 200°C (400°F), Gas 6. Place the chicken in a roasting tin and drizzle with the olive oil, season well with salt

and pepper and roast in the oven for 25 minutes or until golden brown and cooked through. Remove from the oven, leave to cool slightly, then remove and discard the skin and bones and cut into bite-size pieces. Retain the cooking juices. Reduce the oven temperature to 180°C (350°F), Gas 4.

2. In a large frying pan, sauté the onions in the vegetable oil for 5–8 minutes until softened. Add the sweetcorn (drained if tinned, cut from the cob if fresh, defrosted if frozen) and stir.

3. Add the chicken pieces, cooking juices and spinach to the onions and sweetcorn and stir until the spinach has wilted. Stir in the béchamel sauce, season to taste with salt and pepper, mix and leave to cool.

4. Fill the pie case with the cooled chicken mixture and cover with a lid made from the remaining pastry (see steps 3–4 of Crumbly Pastry: Pie Case and Lid on page 127 for a reminder of how to make a pie lid). Bake for 25–30 minutes in the oven until the pastry is golden brown and the filling is piping hot.

Lamb Bolognese
Feeds 4

225g minced lamb
1–2 tbsp vegetable oil
3 onions, sliced
2–3 garlic cloves (to taste), crushed
bunch of flat-leaf parsley, finely chopped
340g cooked Brown Rice (see page 137)
300ml Tomato Sauce (see page 148)
sea salt and freshly ground black pepper

Method

1. In a frying pan, brown the mince in hot oil then add the onions and garlic and sauté for 5 minutes.

2. Add the parsley and sauté for a further 5–10 minutes, then add the cooked rice and tomato sauce, stir and season with salt and pepper.

Liver and Bacon Casserole

Feeds 4. Serve with mashed potato
(see Buttery Mash on page 135) and sautéed greens

You will need a medium casserole dish

2–3 tbsp wholemeal flour
1 tsp mixed herbs
455g lamb's liver, washed, with the outer membrane and any white
    connective tissue removed, and thinly sliced
3 onions, sliced
225g streaky bacon
1 tbsp vegetable oil
1 tbsp Marmite or Vegemite
1 tbsp tomato purée
sea salt and freshly ground black pepper

Method

1. Grease the casserole dish and preheat the oven to 200°C (400°F),
   Gas 6. Put the flour, herbs and salt and pepper in a small plastic
   bag along with the thinly sliced liver and shake until the liver is
   well coated.
2. Place the onions in the casserole, followed by the coated liver.
   Fry the bacon on both sides in the oil for 5 minutes over a
   medium heat and then lay on top of the liver.
3. Place the open casserole dish on the top shelf of the oven and let
   the bacon crisp for 10 minutes.
4. Remove the casserole dish from the oven and reduce the
   temperature to 180°C (350°F), Gas 4. Mix together the Marmite
   or Vegemite and tomato purée with 250ml of boiled water that has
   slightly cooled and pour over the onions, liver and bacon.
5. Cover and bake for a further 40 minutes.

Streaky Bacon and Potato Pie

Feeds 4. Serve with lightly steamed or boiled Brussels sprouts

1 Crumbly Pastry case, blind baked and lining a 24cm round pie dish, 5cm deep, with a third of the pastry left over for the lid (see steps 1–2 of Crumbly Pastry: Pie Case and Lid, page 127)

225g streaky bacon
1 tbsp vegetable oil
4 small onions or 2 large onions, sliced
600ml Basic Béchamel Sauce (see page 146)
freshly grated nutmeg
680g potatoes, boiled in salted water for 10 minutes and thickly sliced
milk, for glazing
sea salt and freshly ground black pepper

Method

1. Preheat the oven to 180°C (350°F), Gas 4. Chop the bacon and fry in the oil on both sides until starting to crisp. Add the onions and fry until lightly golden.
2. Add the béchamel sauce, stir, add the nutmeg and season with salt and pepper.
3. Add the potatoes, stir, then remove from the heat and set aside.
4. Spoon the potato mixture into the blind-baked pastry case. Cover with a thin lid made from the remaining pastry (see steps 3–4 of Crumbly Pastry: Pie Case and Lid on page 127 for a reminder of how to make a pie lid). After chilling the uncooked pie for 10 minutes, bake in the oven for 20 minutes or until the pastry is golden brown.

SALADS

Crisp Green Salad

Feeds 4 as an accompaniment to a main meal

half a lettuce
half a bunch of watercress
1 cucumber, sliced
1 green pepper, deseeded and sliced
4 spring onions, finely sliced
a few green olives

Dressing
1 tsp salt
2 tsp vinegar
1 tsp sunflower oil
sea salt and freshly ground black pepper

Method

1. Rinse and drain the lettuce and watercress. Chop the lettuce, then transfer both the lettuce and watercress to a large salad bowl and add the other ingredients.
2. Mix together all the dressing ingredients and drizzle over the salad just before serving.

Tip for watercress

Sad and limp watercress can be revived by standing it upright in cold water.

Decadent Winter Slaw

Feeds 4. Works well with quiches, pies and flans

225g red cabbage, finely shredded
2 carrots, grated
2 celery sticks, chopped
1 small apple, grated
1 onion, sliced (white or red)
1 tbsp raisins

Dressing

1 tsp salt
1 tbsp malt vinegar
1 tbsp sunflower oil

Method

Combine the vegetables and fruit in a large salad bowl.
Mix the dressing ingredients and pour over the salad.

Vibrant Carrot, Raisin and Rice Salad

Feeds 4 as a robust accompaniment to a main dish

2 carrots, grated
115g white cabbage, shredded
1 small onion, finely chopped
115g cooked peas
1 tbsp raisins
340g cooked Brown Rice (see page 137)

Dressing
1 tsp salt
1 tbsp soy sauce
1 tsp balsamic vinegar
1 tbsp lemon juice
1 tsp mustard powder or Dijon mustard
1–2 tbsp olive oil

Method
Add all the other ingredients to the cooked rice and then season
with the mixed dressing. Delicious served hot or cold.

....

The Original Potato Salad

Feeds 4

900g potatoes, diced
1 onion, chopped
2 celery sticks, chopped
2 Hard-Boiled Eggs (see page 150), sliced
flat-leaf parsley, finely chopped

Dressing

115g cream cheese
1 tbsp sunflower oil
1 tbsp vinegar (any variety will do, but cider vinegar works
　　particularly well)
sea salt and freshly ground black pepper

Method

1. Boil the potatoes until just tender but not soft – for about 7–10
   minutes. Combine with the salad ingredients while hot, then
   add the mixed salad dressing and toss everything together.
2. Serve hot or chilled.

....

Sweet Potato Salad with a Lemon Honey Dressing

Feeds 4 as a light lunch or side dish to a main meal

450g sweet potatoes, scrubbed or peeled, cut into chunks
　　　　and boiled in salted water until tender but not soft
3 spring onions, chopped

Dressing

1 tsp soy sauce
1 tsp lemon juice
1 tsp runny honey
1 tbsp olive oil
sea salt and freshly ground black pepper

Method

Combine the dressing, then mix all of the ingredients in a large
bowl while the sweet potatoes are still hot. Serve hot or chilled.

Crunchy Red Bean and Green Pepper Salad

Feeds 4 as a light lunch or side dish to a main meal

340g red kidney beans, either cooked from dry (see Red
    Kidney Beans on page 138) or tinned, drained
1 green pepper, deseeded and chopped
2 celery sticks, chopped
1 onion, finely chopped
1–2 garlic cloves (to taste), crushed

Dressing
1 tbsp lemon juice
1 tbsp olive oil
sea salt and freshly ground black pepper

Method
Combine the cooked beans with the salad ingredients and the
mixed dressing while still hot. Delicious served hot or chilled.

Curried Rice Salad

Feeds 4

340g cooked Brown Rice (see page 137)
1 green pepper, deseeded and chopped
2 celery sticks, chopped
2 carrots, grated
1 small onion, finely chopped
1 small apple, grated

Dressing

1 tsp salt
1 tbsp soy sauce
1 tsp apple cider vinegar
1 tbsp lemon juice
2–3 tsp curry powder
1 tbsp sunflower oil

Method

Add the salad ingredients to the warm, cooked rice and season
with the mixed dressing. Serve hot or cold.

....

Marinated Mackerel with Fresh Greens and a Zingy Mustard Dressing

Feeds 4 as a healthy and hearty lunch

1 medium mackerel, fresh (if possible)
half a round lettuce
bunch of watercress, chopped
1 onion, finely chopped
1 carrot, grated
chunk of cucumber, sliced
a few green or black olives

Dressing

1 tbsp lemon juice
1 tsp mustard powder
1 tbsp vegetable oil
sea salt and freshly ground black pepper

Method

1. If not using filleted fish, bake in a preheated oven at 180°C (350°F), Gas 4 for about 15–20 minutes then remove bones. If filleted, sauté until beginning to flake.
2. Marinate the fish for up to 1 hour in the mixed dressing. Add the salad ingredients just before serving and toss well.

Chicken and Spring Onion Salad with a Yoghurt and Lime Dressing

Feeds 4

2 chicken pieces, cooked
2 carrots, grated
1 green pepper, deseeded and sliced
3 spring onions, chopped
2 celery sticks, chopped
50g chestnut or button mushrooms, sliced
3 tomatoes, sliced

Dressing

150g carton of natural yoghurt
4 tbsp single cream
1 tbsp lime juice
1 tbsp sunflower oil
1 tsp mustard powder or wholegrain mustard
salt and freshly ground black pepper

Method

Remove the chicken meat from the bone if necessary and shred then combine with the salad ingredients and the mixed yoghurt dressing. Serve chilled.

DESSERTS

Bread and Butter Pudding

Feeds 4

You will need a medium ovenproof pie dish

6 slices of wholemeal bread, buttered
115g sultanas
2 eggs
55g soft light brown sugar
570ml milk

Method

1. Preheat the oven 180°C (350°F), Gas 4. Arrange layers of bread and sultanas, ending with a layer of bread, in a greased pie dish (bread should only half fill the dish).
2. Beat together the eggs, sugar and milk and pour over the bread.
3. Bake for 40–50 minutes until crisp and golden.

Honey Rice Pudding

Feeds 4

You will need a medium ovenproof pie or gratin dish

170g cooked white rice
500ml milk
1 tbsp runny honey
25g butter or margarine
1 egg, beaten
1 drop of vanilla essence
1 tsp soft light brown sugar mixed with 1 tsp mixed spice

Method

1. Preheat the oven to 150°C (300°F), Gas 2. Simmer the rice in milk for 10–15 minutes, stirring regularly.
2. Remove from the heat and stir in the honey and butter.
3. Leave to cool slightly for 10–15 minutes, stirring often.
4. When cool, gently stir in the beaten egg and add a drop of vanilla essence.
5. Turn into a buttered dish and sprinkle with the sugar and spice mix.
6. Bake in the oven for 30–40 minutes until golden brown on top. Leave to stand for at least 5–10 minutes before serving.

Apple and Rhubarb Crumble

*Feeds 4. Delicious with custard,
ice cream, yoghurt or cream*

You will need a shallow ovenproof dish

455g cooking apples, peeled, cored and chopped
250g rhubarb, chopped
1 tbsp soft light brown sugar

Topping
115g butter or sunflower margarine
170g plain wholemeal flour
170g porridge oats
85g soft light brown sugar
1–2 tbsp sunflower oil

Method
1. Preheat the oven to 190°C (375°F), Gas 5. Place the apples and rhubarb in a shallow ovenproof dish, packing the slices in tightly.
2. Sprinkle with the brown sugar and add 100–150ml of water.
3. To make the crumble topping rub the butter into the dry ingredients. Add the sunflower oil and mix until crumbly.
4. Sprinkle the crumble over the fruit and bake in the oven for about 30 minutes or until the fruit starts to bubble up and the crumble topping turns brown.

Apple and Blackberry Pie

Feeds 4. Serve with custard,
cream, ice cream or yoghurt

1 Crumbly Pastry case, blind baked and lining a 24cm round
ovenproof pie dish, 5cm deep, with a third of the pastry left over for
the lid (see steps 1–2 of Crumbly Pastry: Pie Case and Lid, page 127)

milk, for brushing

Filling
455g cooking apples, peeled, cored and quartered
250g blackberries
2 tbsp soft light brown sugar

Method
1. Preheat the oven to 170°C (325°F), Gas 3. Place the apples and
   blackberries in the blind-baked pastry case and sprinkle them
   with sugar and 3–4 tablespoons of water.
2. Cover with a lid made from the remaining pastry (see steps 3–4
   of Crumbly Pastry: Pie Case and Lid on page 127 for a reminder
   of how to make a pie lid).
3. Bake on the middle shelf of the oven for 30 minutes until the
   pastry is golden brown and the fruit is starting to simmer.

– ALTERNATIVELY –

These combinations also make good fruit pies. Use roughly
the same amount of fruit as in the Apple and Blackberry Pie:
○ Apple and raisins with cinnamon
○ Rhubarb and lemon
○ Gooseberry and banana

Baked Apples
Feeds 4

You will need an ovenproof dish

4 medium cooking apples
2 tbsp soft light brown sugar
knob of butter or margarine

Method
1. Preheat the oven to 200°C (400°F), Gas 6. Core each apple and stand them in an ovenproof dish with 4 tablespoons of water.
2. Fill each apple core with sugar and top with a small knob of butter. Bake in the ovenproof dish for about 45 minutes until the apples are soft.

– ALTERNATIVELY –

Apple Dumplings

Method
1. Stuff the cored apples with mincemeat, dried fruit, dates and/or chopped nuts.
2. Make 460g of Sweet Wholemeal Shortcrust Pastry dough (see step 1 on page 129).
3. Divide the pastry into 4 pieces, and on a floured surface roll each piece into a circle 20–25cm across.
4. Completely cover the stuffed apples with the shortcrust pastry rounds, adding 1–2 teaspoons of water in each core just before sealing the pastry.
5. Bake at 180°C (350°F), Gas 4 for 45–60 minutes, until the pastry is golden and the apple is bubbling.

Eve's Pudding

Feeds 4

You will need an ovenproof dish

Topping
85g butter or margarine
85g caster sugar
1 egg, beaten
140g self-raising white flour
a drop of milk, for mixing

Filling
450g cooking apples
85g soft light brown sugar
grated zest of 1 lemon

Method
1. Preheat the oven to 180°C (350°F), Gas 4. To make the topping, cream the butter or margarine and sugar together until pale and fluffy. Add the egg a little at a time, beating well after each addition until well blended.
2. Gradually fold in the flour and add enough milk to give a dropping consistency. (The mixture should fall off the wooden spoon quite easily when shaken.)
3. To make the filling, slice and core the apples and place in a greased ovenproof dish. Sprinkle the brown sugar and lemon zest over the apples and drizzle with 1–2 teaspoons of water.
4. Spread the topping mixture over the apples. Bake for 40–45 minutes until the apples are tender and the sponge is golden.

Treacle Tart

Feeds 4–6. Serve with a dollop of vanilla ice cream

240g Sweet Wholemeal Shortcrust Pastry base lining a 20cm round flan tin, 2cm deep, not blind baked (use the quantities below to make 240g of dough; see steps 1–2 on page 129 for the method. Remember to save the excess pastry for the lattice decoration)

55g self-raising wholemeal flour
85g plain white flour
20g soft light brown sugar
50g cold unsalted butter or margarine
1 tbsp sunflower oil
1 tbsp cold water

Filling
225g golden syrup
finely grated zest and juice of 1 lemon
75g breadcrumbs
1 egg, beaten, for glazing

Method
1. Preheat the oven to 190°C (375°F), Gas 5. To make the filling, warm the golden syrup in a saucepan with the lemon zest and juice. Sprinkle the breadcrumbs into the syrup, stir and slowly pour into the pastry case.
2. Make strips from the pastry trimmings and make a lattice pattern over the tart. Brush the ends with water to stick them to the pastry case. Glaze the pastry strips with the beaten egg.
3. Place the tart on a baking tray and bake in the oven for 20–25 minutes until the filling is just set.

Wholefruit Cake

Feeds 6

You will need a 25cm round cake tin

170g soft light brown sugar
85g margarine
455g dried fruit
1 tsp mixed spice
1 level tsp bicarbonate of soda
2 eggs
455g self-raising wholemeal flour

Method

1. Preheat the oven to 170°C (325°F), Gas 3. Put all the ingredients except the eggs and the flour into a saucepan. Add 570ml of cold water and bring to the boil. Remove from the heat, stir and cover. Leave to cool for 1 hour at room temperature.
2. When cool, beat in the eggs and gradually stir in the flour.
3. Turn into a greased cake tin and bake for 1½–2 hours, or until a knife inserted into the middle comes out clean.

Tip

To freshen stale cake put the cake in a pudding basin, cover with a lid or plate and steam for 30 minutes.

Black Treacle Flapjacks

Makes 12

You will need a shallow 25cm square baking tin

140g butter or sunflower margarine
85g soft light brown sugar
1 tbsp molasses or black treacle
225g rolled oats

Method

1. Melt the butter or margarine, brown sugar and molasses slowly in a large saucepan. Add the oats and combine, then spread into an oiled shallow round baking tin and bake at 190°C (375°F), Gas 5 for 20–25 minutes.
2. Mark into squares while still hot and remove from the tin when cold.

....

Wholemeal Sultana Scones

Makes 10

225g plain wholemeal flour
1 heaped tsp baking powder
pinch of salt
1 tbsp caster sugar
50g butter or margarine
50g sultanas
150ml milk
1 egg, beaten, for glazing

Method
1. Preheat the oven to 220°C (425°F), Gas 7. Mix the flour, baking powder, salt and sugar. Rub in the butter until the mixture resembles breadcrumbs.
2. Add the sultanas and the milk and stir to make a soft dough. Knead lightly on a floured surface to make a ball, then roll out to 2cm thick and cut out about 10 rounds.
3. Transfer them to a greased baking sheet, brush with the beaten egg or some milk and bake for 15–20 minutes until brown and well risen.

Peanut Butter, Oat and Raisin Cookies

Makes about 12–15

115g butter or margarine
85g soft light brown sugar
115g crunchy peanut butter
115g rolled oats
115g self-raising wholemeal flour
55g raisins
1 tsp bicarbonate of soda

Method
1. Preheat the oven to 180°C (350°F), Gas 4. Melt the butter or margarine and brown sugar in a saucepan. Stir in the peanut butter, oats, flour, raisins and bicarbonate of soda and mix well.
2. Place spoonfuls of the mixture onto a greased baking sheet. Bake in the middle of the oven for 20 minutes until golden brown.

Mama's Sweet Potato Pie

Feeds 4. Serve hot or cold with ice cream

1 Sweet Wholemeal Shortcrust Pastry base, lining a 23–25cm,
3–4cm deep round flan tin or pie dish (see steps 1–4 on page 129)

Filling
500g mashed sweet potatoes (see page 136 for Sweet Potato Mash,
    but don't add oil or seasoning)
100g soft dark brown sugar
1 tsp mixed spice
pinch of salt
4 egg yolks, beaten
90g butter or margarine, melted
450ml milk
4 egg whites, whisked until beginning to form stiff peaks

Method
1. Preheat the oven to 220°C (425°F), Gas 7. To make the filling,
   mix together the mashed sweet potatoes, brown sugar, mixed
   spice and salt in a large bowl until combined, then add the
   beaten egg yolks and melted butter.
2. Mix well and gradually add the milk, stirring with a wooden spoon.
3. Fold the sweet potato mixture into the egg whites.
4. Pour the mixture into the sweet flan base and bake for 15 minutes.
5. Reduce heat to 190°C (375°F), Gas 5 and bake for 25–30 minutes
   until brown and firm.

Potato Cheesecake

Feeds 8. Don't be put off by the white potatoes in this recipe.
Potato Cheesecake is delicious hot or cold with yoghurt,
cream or ice cream, or just on its own

1 Sweet Wholemeal Shortcrust Pastry base, lining a 23–25cm,
3–4cm deep loose-bottomed round flan tin or pie dish (see page
129), not blind baked

Filling

115g butter or margarine
115g caster sugar
3 eggs, beaten
115g sultanas or currants
550g mashed potato (for a reminder of how to make mashed
potato, see Buttery Mash on page 135, but don't add butter
or seasoning) zest and juice of 1 small lemon

Method

1. Preheat the oven to 190°C (375°F), Gas 5. Beat the butter and
   sugar together until pale and creamy. Add the eggs gradually,
   beating after each addition until smooth.
2. Fold in the sultanas or currants, mashed potato and lemon juice.
3. Fill the pastry base with the potato mixture and bake for
   approximately 1 hour until set and golden brown. This cheesecake
   will keep in the fridge for up to 2 days.

BASIC ESSENTIALS

Bargain Bread

Makes 2 large 1kg loaves

You will need 2 large loaf tins, approximately 18 x 9cm at the base and 7cm deep

2 tsp sugar
5 tsp dried active yeast
1.4kg strong wholemeal flour
3 tsp salt

Method

1. Turn the oven to its lowest setting to warm up. Gently heat 850ml of cold water in a saucepan until it becomes hand-hot.
2. In a jug, dissolve the sugar in 4 tablespoons of the warmed water and then add the yeast. Leave to froth in a warm place for 10–15 minutes.

3. Meanwhile, grease and flour 2 large loaf tins and measure the flour and salt into a large bowl. Add the yeast mixture and then gradually add the rest of the water and mix to a dough.

4. Knead on a floured worksurface for 10–15 minutes, adding more water or flour as necessary, to make a dough that is smooth, elastic and not sticky. Turn off the oven. Divide the dough into 2, shape and place in the loaf tins. Cover loosely with cling film and leave to rise in the warm oven for approximately 30 minutes, or until they have risen 2.5cm above the tins, then remove.

5. Turn the oven up to 200°C (400°F), Gas 6 and once the correct temperature is reached, bake the loaves for about 40 minutes or until brown on top.

6. Turn the loaves out of the tins. Check the loaves are cooked by tapping the base. They should sound hollow. Allow to cool on a wire rack.

– ALTERNATIVELY –

Bread Buns

If short of suitable tins for making loaves, bread buns are quick and practical. Halve the quantities of the Bargain Bread ingredients and follow the recipe but instead of putting into loaf tins, shape the dough into 10 bread buns. Place them on a greased baking sheet and leave them to rise in the warm oven or another warm place for 15–20 minutes or until they are twice their size. Bake at 200°C (400°F), Gas 6 on a low shelf in the oven for 25 minutes.

Honey – Milk Toast

Feeds 4

6 slices of wholemeal bread
15g butter or margarine
570ml hot milk
1 tbsp runny honey or soft dark brown sugar

Method

1. Toast, lightly butter and dice the bread. Divide into serving bowls.
2. Sweeten the milk with honey or brown sugar then pour over the toast cubes. Serve hot.

– ALTERNATIVELY –

○ Try with hot chocolate milk or honey-vanilla milk.
○ Serve chilled in the summer.

....

Heidi Breakfast

Feeds 4

6 slices of wholemeal bread, toasted
6 tbsp raisins or sultanas
handful of strawberries, sliced
3 tsp soft light brown sugar (optional)
570ml milk or yoghurt
2 bananas, peeled and sliced (optional)

Method

1. Dice and divide the toast into serving bowls. Sprinkle with raisins or sultanas, strawberries and, if desired, brown sugar.
2. Serve with milk or yoghurt and sliced banana, if desired.

Tip
Stale bread can be freshened if brushed entirely in milk and baked moderately for 15 minutes. The crust will be crispened and the inside nicer than otherwise.

....

Raisin Bread

Makes 2 large 1kg loaves

You will need 2 loaf tins, approximately 18 x 9cm at the base and 7cm deep

2–3 level tbsp soft light brown sugar
6 tsp dried active yeast
1.4kg strong wholemeal flour
1 tsp salt
280g raisins
4 tbsp vegetable oil (optional)

Glaze
1 egg
1 tbsp soft light brown sugar
2 tbsp milk

Method
1. Turn the oven to its lowest setting to warm up. Gently heat 850ml of cold water in a saucepan until it becomes hand-hot. In a jug, dissolve the sugar in 4 tablespoons of the warmed water, then add the yeast and leave in a warm place to froth for 10–15 minutes.
2. Mix the flour, salt and raisins together and add the yeast mixture. Knead and gradually add the rest of the water and the oil to form a dough.
3. Follow steps 4–6 for Bargain Bread (see page 120) and, if liked, brush the loaf with the combined glaze before baking.

Bernie's Easy Bread

Makes 2 medium 900g loaves or 24 small rolls

You will need 2 loaf tins, approximately 18 x 9cm at the base and 7cm deep

800g plain wholemeal flour
200g strong white flour (or, if you don't have any around, plain
    white flour will do)
2 tsp caster sugar
2 tsp salt
2 x 7g packets of fast-action yeast
1–2 tbsp vegetable oil or olive oil

Method

1. Turn the oven to its lowest setting to warm up. Gently heat
   700ml of cold water in a saucepan until it becomes hand-hot.
2. Mix the flours, sugar, salt and yeast together in a large bowl and
   make a well in the middle. Add the warm water into the well and
   combine with a wooden spoon. Add the oil and bring into a ball.
3. Turn out onto a lightly floured worksurface and knead for
   approximately 10 minutes until the dough is no longer sticky.
   Add a little more flour as necessary until the dough is not sticky
   and slightly springy to the touch.
4. Place the dough in a lightly oiled bowl and leave to rise in a warm
   place for 1 hour or until doubled in size. Then divide into 2 and
   place in the loaf tins, cover with cling film and leave to rise in
   the warm oven or in another warm place for 45–60 minutes.
   Alternatively, shape the dough into buns, place on a baking sheet
   lined with baking paper and leave to rise for 45–60 minutes or until
   doubled in size. If desired, score the dough across the top with a
   sharp knife, brush the top with beaten egg or milk to make it glossy,
   and sprinkle with rolled oats or sesame, sunflower or poppy seeds.
5. Increase the oven temperature to 200°C (400°F), Gas 6 and bake
   for 30–40 minutes, or for just 20 minutes if making buns.

PASTRY

Tips for Pastry

1. If the dough crumbles when being rolled out, don't panic. Knead it again with a drop more water.
2. If the dough is too sticky, add a little more flour.
3. If the dough starts to fragment when rolled onto the rolling pin before being brought to the dish or tin, transfer the remaining pastry left on the rolling pin to the flan tin and mould on the rest after moistening it a little.
4. After lining your dish or tin with pastry, if you seem a little short of dough, use the trimmings from around the edge of the tin to patch up the pastry case. And if you are still a little short, no sweat – the pastry case will be a little uneven but it will taste just as nice!
5. Keep surplus pastry in a plastic sandwich bag in the fridge. It will keep for 2–3 days.

Wholemeal Pastry

Some people are wary about using wholemeal flour in pastry. They find it grainy and heavy and when it comes to rolling it out, it doesn't hold in one piece. Then, to top it all, after baking, it seems so hard and crunchy by comparison to pastry made using white flour. But it's merely a matter of becoming accustomed to the difference.

Once you have kneaded a good dough – not too sticky or too dry – you should find it comparatively easy to roll out.

Wholemeal Flan Pastry

Makes 370g, enough for 1 medium flan or quiche

This recipe works for a 22cm round flan dish, 4cm deep

115g butter or margarine, or 90ml sunflower oil
225g plain wholemeal flour

Method

1. Preheat the oven to 190°C (375°F), Gas 5. Rub the butter into the flour until the mixture resembles fine breadcrumbs or, if using oil, stir the oil into the flour with a round-bladed knife. Add a little cold water and knead into a dough.
2. Roll the pastry out evenly on a floured surface. To line the flan case, roll the pastry up onto the rolling pin and unroll it over the flan tin.
3. Gently lower the pastry into the tin, then press it firmly into the edges. Repair any cracks.
4. Roll a rolling pin over the rim of the tin to get rid of any excess pastry. Prick the base of the flan with a fork and line with greaseproof paper or foil, then fill with dried beans, rice or pastry weights. Bake blind in the oven for 10–15 minutes.
5. Remove the beans and greaseproof paper and return to the oven for a further 5 minutes or until the case is cooked through.

To bake blind means to fully bake a pastry case without a filling.

Use Wholemeal Flan Pastry in the Cheddar and Sautéed Onion Quiche on page 53, Sautéed Onion, Tomato and Red Split Lentil Tart on page 60 and Potato, Cheddar and Onion Tart with Spring Greens on page 59.

Crumbly Pastry
(For pies and pasties)

Makes 340g, enough for 6 pasties or 1 savoury medium pie case

This recipe works for a 24cm round flan tin or pie dish, 5cm deep, with a 17cm base

170g cold butter or margarine, cubed
225g self-raising wholemeal flour
115g plain white flour
pinch of sea salt
4 tbsp milk, and extra for glazing

....

Pie Case and Lid

Method

1. Preheat the oven to 200°C (400°F), Gas 6. Rub the butter or margarine into the flours and salt until the mixture resembles fine breadcrumbs. Gradually add 4 tablespoons of milk and knead to a dough. Roll into a ball, wrap in cling film and chill for at least 10 minutes, then break away a third of the dough and set aside – this will be the pie lid. Roll out the remaining larger piece of pastry evenly on a floured worksurface, until it is the thickness of a £1 coin.

2. To line the pie dish, roll the pastry up onto the rolling pin and unroll it over the dish. Gently lower the pastry into the dish, then press it firmly into the corners and edges. Prick the base with a fork, line with baking paper and baking beans or pastry weights and chill in the fridge for another 10 minutes. Place the pie base into the preheated oven and blind bake for 15 minutes. Remove the baking beans and paper and bake for a further 5 minutes or

until the base of the pastry is firm. Remove from the oven and leave to cool.

3. Once the pie filling has been made and transferred to the prepared pastry-lined pie dish, roll out the remaining pastry set side earlier on a floured worksurface to make the lid. As before, roll the pastry up onto the rolling pin and unroll it over the dish. Brush the edges of the pastry case with milk or water and press the edges of the lid down on the pastry case to seal.

4. Brush the top with milk and chill the uncooked pie for 10 minutes. Bake in a preheated oven at the temperature and for the time specified in the pie recipe until the pastry is golden brown.

Pasties

Method

1. Rub the butter or margarine into the flours and salt until the mixture resembles fine breadcrumbs. Gradually add 4 tablespoons of cold water or milk and knead to a dough.

2. With floured hands, roll the pastry into a long sausage shape, wrap in cling film and chill for at least 10 minutes. Divide the sausage into 6 pieces and roll each one out to form a circle. Sprinkle them with flour and leave ready to fill. Make your filling. Be inventive, this is a good opportunity to use up leftover meat and vegetables

3. Put a spoonful of the filling onto one side of each circle. Dampen the edges of each circle with a little milk, then fold the pastry over the filling to make a semi-circle and press the edges together so that the filling cannot escape. Trim the edge of the semi-circle with a sharp knife to neaten, then press with a fork to seal the edges tightly.

4. Make a small hole in the top of each pasty to allow the steam to escape and brush with milk. Place on a baking sheet lined with baking paper and chill for at least 10 minutes.

5. Bake in the oven at 180°C (350°F), Gas 4 for 25–30 minutes (depending on the filling) or until golden brown on top and the pastry is crisp. Serve with a large green salad.

Use Crumbly Pastry in Root Vegetable Pie on page 57, Wilted Spinach, Potato and Sweetcorn Pie on page 58, Spinach Pasties with Cream Cheese and Mash on page 63, Chicken and Sweetcorn Pie on page 97, Streaky Bacon and Potato Pie on page 100 and Apple and Blackberry Pie on page 111.

....

Sweet Wholemeal Shortcrust Pastry

Makes 460g, enough for 1 dessert pie case. Make in a 23–25cm, 3–4cm deep round flan tin or pie dish

This recipe includes blind baking, but this step isn't strictly necessary for all recipes using the shortcrust pastry case – the wetter the filling, the greater the need to blind bake

115g self-raising wholemeal flour
170g plain white flour
55g caster sugar
115g cold unsalted butter or margarine
2 tbsp sunflower oil

Method
1. Preheat the oven to 200°C (400°F), Gas 3. Mix together the flours and the sugar and quickly rub in the butter or margarine (try not to take too long as this pastry should stay as cool as possible). Add the oil and 2 tablespoons of cold water and mix to a dough. Roll into a ball, wrap in cling film and leave in the fridge for 30 minutes. Roll the pastry out evenly on a floured surface. To line the tin or

dish, roll the pastry up onto the rolling pin and unroll it over the flan tin. Gently lower the pastry into the tin, then press it firmly into the corners and edges.
2. Roll a rolling pin over the rim of the tin to get rid of any excess pastry.
3. Prick the base of the flan with a fork and line with greaseproof paper or foil, then fill with dried beans, rice or pastry weights. Bake blind in the oven at the specified temperature for 10–15 minutes.
4. Remove the beans and greaseproof paper and return to the oven for a further 5 minutes or until the case is cooked through.

Use Sweet Wholemeal Shortcrust Pastry in Potato Cheesecake on page 119, Mama's Sweet Potato Pie on page 118 and Treacle Tart on page 114.

Butter Dumplings

*Makes 6. Dumplings need not be savoury,
and can be served with fruit sauce or jam*

55g cold butter
115g self-raising wholemeal flour

Method

1. Rub the butter into the flour until the mixture begins to resemble breadcrumbs, then add just enough cold water to form a stiffish dough.
2. Roll the dough into small balls and place on top of an almost-ready simmering soup or casserole (arranged around the edge, as dumplings in the middle take longer to cook), cover and cook for 1–12 minutes until swollen. (Alternatively, boil in salted water for 1–12 minutes.)
3. Serve immediately as dumplings left immersed for too long become heavy.

Chapatis or Flatbread

Makes 6–8 small chapatis. These chapatis are incredibly easy to make and much cheaper than shop-bought flour tortillas. Ideal with curries and stews

225g self-raising wholemeal flour
1 tsp salt
3–4 tbsp sunflower oil

Method

1. Form a dough with the flour, salt and a little cold water, adding the water gradually. Knead until smooth and soft.
2. Make 6–8 balls from the dough and flatten them to form patty shapes. Roll out thinly on a floured surface. Coat each chapati with flour on both sides.
3. Fry in a little oil on both sides until golden and crispy. Keep warm in the oven on its lowest setting until the rest are cooked.

– ALTERNATIVELY –

° If you don't have enough wholemeal flour, or if you prefer your chapatis slightly chewier, you can use self-raising white flour instead, or a mixture of both flours.

Quick Raisin Bread

By adding a few raisins and a little sugar to the dough, a quick raisin bread can also be made.

Johnny Cakes

These little savoury cakes are great for using up any leftover ingredients like fish, onions, tomatoes, chicken, cheese, spinach, peppers – you name it!

Follow the recipe for Chapatis or Flatbread (see page 131), adding any leftover ingredients you may have to the dough, but don't roll them out. Form into small cakes, like scones, and fry on both sides in hot oil in a large, heavy pan until browned. Serve hot or cold – they make great lunchbox snacks.

Polenta Pastry

Makes 300g. Great for an alternative pizza base

115g plain white flour
70g fine polenta
2 tbsp baking powder
pinch of salt
2–3 tbsp sunflower oil

Method
1. Mix together the dry ingredients in a large bowl.
2. Make a well and add 140ml of cold water and the oil.
3. Mix together and knead for about 6–8 minutes until the dough is stretchy. Add the toppings, then pop in the oven at the highest temperature for 12–15 minutes for a quick pizza.

Jacket Potatoes

Convenient, easy, wholesome and they make economical use of the oven – a vacant top shelf being perfect for a large trayful of spuds. The skin is full of fibre and vitamin C. Make a meal with the simple addition of beans, cheese, tuna and salad.

1–2 medium potatoes per person (the King Edward, Maris Piper, Wilja, Ailsa, Golden Wonder and Marfona varieties are all particularly well-suited to baking, but you can use whatever you have knocking about in the cupboard)
butter or sunflower oil, for brushing
sea salt and freshly ground black pepper

Method
1. Preheat the oven to 200°C (400°F), Gas 6. Wash and scrub each potato, remove any bad parts and prick with a fork. Brush the potatoes with melted butter or oil and cover with sea salt for crisp skins.
2. Place on a baking tray on the top shelf of the oven and bake for 45–60 minutes, possibly more or less depending on the size of the potatoes, until cooked right through. They are done when you can make a slight dent in the skin when applying light pressure.
3. Split in half and serve hot with butter, sea salt and freshly ground black pepper.

Roast Potatoes

Feeds 4 as a classic partner to a roast

500g potatoes (Desirée, Romano, Maris Piper or King Edward
    varieties produce the best results but you can use any)
60g butter or 2 tbsp vegetable oil
sea salt and freshly ground black pepper

Method

1. Preheat the oven to 220°C, (425°F), Gas 7. Scrub the potatoes or
   peel if preferred. Cut them into even-sized chunks and boil in a
   pan of salted water for 3 minutes, then drain.
2. Place them with the butter or oil in a roasting tin or around a
   meat joint or nut roast. Roughly toss the potatoes in the butter or
   oil until covered.
3. Cook in the oven for 45–60 minutes, turning once or twice until
   golden all over, crisp on the outside and fluffy on the inside.
4. Season with salt and pepper 5 minutes before serving.

New Potatoes with Dill

Feeds 4 as a side dish

500g new potatoes
1 tsp salt
1 tbsp butter or olive oil
1 tbsp finely chopped dill

Method

1. Wash the potatoes and cut them into halves or quarters, depending
   on their size.

2. Place them in a saucepan with enough cold water to cover them and add the salt.
3. Bring to the boil then simmer for about 15 minutes until tender.
4. Drain the potatoes, add the butter or oil and chopped dill and mix, so that the potates have a golden glaze flecked with dill.

– ALTERNATIVELY –

° Use chopped flat-leaf parsley, mint or chives instead of dill.

....

Buttery Mash

Feeds 4, as an accompaniment to a main meal,
or as an adequately comforting dish in its own right

500g potatoes, scrubbed or peeled and diced (the King Edward
　　　or Maris Piper varieties make a reliably good mash)
55g butter or margarine
sea salt and freshly ground black pepper

Method
1. Bring the potatoes to the boil in a pan of salted water and simmer for 10–15 minutes until tender.
2. Drain and mash the potatoes with a potato masher. Add the butter and blend with a fork until fluffy.
3. Season to taste with salt and pepper.

– ALTERNATIVELY –

Sweet Potato Mash

Feeds 4

500g sweet potatoes, scrubbed or peeled and diced
1 tbsp olive oil
sea salt and freshly ground black pepper

Method

1. Place the diced sweet potatoes in a large saucepan with enough boiling salted water to cover them.
2. Boil for 15 minutes or until tender. With a potato masher, mash the potatoes with the olive oil and season with salt and pepper.

....

Chunky Oven Chips

Feeds 4 as a tasty snack or part of a main meal

500g potatoes, peeled or scrubbed (Desirée, Maris Piper or King Edward work well, but any will do)
1–2 tbsp vegetable oil
sea salt and freshly ground black pepper

Method

1. Preheat the oven to 200°C (400°F), Gas 6. Cut the potatoes into chunky chip shapes.
2. Rest the raw chips on kitchen paper to dry out slightly for 5 minutes. Spread the chips over a baking tray or roasting tin, drizzle with oil, then season with salt and pepper. Toss them about to make sure they're evenly coated.
3. Roast for 45–50 minutes, turning over once or twice, until crisp and golden on the outside and fluffy on the inside.

– ALTERNATIVELY –

Spicy

Combine 1 teaspoon of paprika, a pinch of chilli flakes, sea salt and freshly ground black pepper and sprinkle over the chips before roasting.

Garlic and herb

Combine 1–3 crushed garlic cloves to taste, 1–2 tablespoons of freshly chopped herbs (or 1–2 teaspoons of dried mixed herbs if you have no fresh herbs to hand) and 1–2 tablespoons of olive oil. Scatter evenly over the chips before roasting.

....

Brown Rice

I first came across brown rice in the mid 1970s when I was living in Notting Hill and wholefoods were all the rage. I studied Macrobiotics and we were encouraged to eat nothing but brown rice for 2 weeks, at the end of which we would reach some sort of epiphany – what sort they didn't say.

I tried but only managed a few days and had to succumb to the added pleasures of sautéed vegetables, fried beans and fish, but found myself already in love with brown rice.

I put that down to the balance of protein, fibre and B vitamins and minerals including B1, B2, B3, B5, B6, B9, iron, magnesium and zinc – good for the nervous system, brain function and the production of feel-good hormones. It's also hugely versatile and can be paired with almost anything.

At first, I didn't add enough water and it was too chewy – a lot of people make the same mistake and some restaurants prefer it that way, but I like mine cooked through with the water gone and the grain burst, but still firm and just starting to stick to the bottom of the pan.

Perfect Brown Rice

Feeds 4 as part of a main meal

340g brown rice
pinch of salt

Method

1. Rinse the rice in a seive under cold running water, place in a large saucepan and cover with 1 litre of cold water and a pinch of salt.
2. Bring to the boil and simmer for 5 minutes without a lid, then cover and simmer gently for about 15–20 minutes until soft and chewy, but not mushy.
3. To test, stick a fork in the rice and if it's starting to stick to the bottom of the pan and the fork emerges with cooked grains stuck to it, it's ready!
4. If the rice is almost cooked and there's plenty of liquid in the pan, cook with the lid off until the liquid has evaporated, or drain (saving the liquid for stock) and cook.
5. If the rice is not cooked but is sticking to the bottom of the pan, add about 140ml of water, cover and cook until ready.

....

Red Kidney Beans

It's important to cook red kidney beans thoroughly or they will cause stomach upsets. Avoid adding any salt to the beans until they are cooked or they will never become tender. You can always buy tinned red kidney beans of course, but buying dried beans in bulk can help you make some significant savings over time, and cooked dried beans are generally considered to taste that bit better than pre-cooked tinned.

Feeds 4 as part of a main meal

340g dried red kidney beans
salt, to taste

Method 1

1. Completely cover the kidney beans in 1.75 litres of cold water and leave to soak overnight. Drain.
2. Simmer in 1.75 litres of fresh cold water, enough to cover them, in a pan with a tight-fitting lid for 1½ hours, or pressure cook at 15psi for 15 minutes. Season with salt only after cooking.

Method 2

1. Soak the kidney beans for at least 4 hours in 1.75 litres of cold water, then drain.
2. Cover the beans with 1.75 litres of fresh cold water and bring to the boil, then continue to boil vigorously for 10 minutes.
3. Cover the pan with the lid and simmer for 1½–2 hours until tender.
4. Break a bean in half to test. If it's still hard in the centre, simmer for a further 30 minutes, adding more water if necessary. I like to cook mine until the starch grain has burst and they're quite soft, but you may like more of a bite to your bean. Season with salt only after the beans have cooked.

....

Black-Eyed Beans

As with kidney beans, you can easily find tinned versions of these beans, but cooked dried ones are cheaper and tend to taste better.

Feeds 4 as part of a main meal

340g black-eyed beans
salt, to taste

Method

1. In a large saucepan, cover the beans with 1.4 litres of cold water and bring to the boil for 10 minutes. Cover with a lid and simmer for 30–40 minutes until tender.
2. Season with salt only once the beans are cooked.

....

Red Split Lentils

Lentils are high in fibre, a great source of protein, cheap and incredibly versatile, and with the addition of some light seasoning, make a delicious addition to more lunches and dinners than you might think. They require different proportions of cooking water depending on what they will be used for, but the cooking method is virtually the same regardless of where they end up.

Feeds 4 . For use in soups

340g red split lentils
1.4 litres cold water
sea salt and freshly ground black pepper

Feeds 4. For use in flans and loaves

340g red split lentils
585ml cold water
sea salt and freshly ground black pepper

Method

1. Bring the lentils to the boil, being careful not to let the saucepan boil over as it forms quite a frothy head. Skim off the froth with a slotted spoon.
2. Reduce the heat. For lentils intended for soups, cover the saucepan with a lid, but leave without a lid for lentils to be used in other

recipes, then simmer gently for 20–30 minutes until firm but tender. Drain. The lentils should be seasoned with salt and pepper liberally, but only after cooking. Fresh herbs, vinegars and lemon juice also all work well.

If…

If, after 30 minutes, the lentils are watery (more of a concern if you want to include them in flans, salads or loaves), keep cooking and stir with a wooden spoon until the liquid has reduced. The lentils will become firmer when removed from the heat and allowed to cool.

If the lentils are too dry, add a drop more water and simmer until tender and plump, stirring with a wooden spoon.

BATTERS FOR PUDDINGS AND PANCAKES

Pouring batter
Yorkshire pudding batter and pancake batter have the consistency of single cream, which makes them ideal for baked batter puddings like Toad in the Hole.

Coating batter
Coating batter is much thicker, like double cream, and made with half the amount of milk. It's perfect for fritters because it clings easily to fruit like bananas or vegetables like mushrooms and is ideal for using up leftovers. This batter is slso good for coating fish or prawns.

Yorkshire Pudding

Feeds 4–6. Perfect with a roast

You will need a rectangular baking tin, around 27 x 20cm, or a tray of individual pudding moulds

115g plain white flour
pinch of salt
1 egg
250ml milk
25g beef dripping or 2 tbsp vegetable or sunflower oil

Method

1. Preheat the oven to 220°C (425°F), Gas 7. Mix the flour and salt in a bowl, make a well in the centre and break in the egg. Beat the mixture with a fork to combine.
2. Add the milk gradually, beating constantly, until the batter is smooth and tiny bubbles have formed on the surface.
3. Put 1cm of dripping or oil in your rectangular baking tin to make 1 large pudding, or in each pudding mould for individual Yorkshire puddings, and place in the oven for about 10 minutes until smoking hot.
4. Pour in the batter and bake in the hot oven for 40–45 minutes if using a baking tin, or 15–20 minutes if using individual pudding moulds, until risen and golden brown. Do not open the oven door during cooking and, if you want to prevent sinking, do not open the oven door until 30 minutes after the pudding is cooked.

– ALTERNATIVELY –

Toad in the Hole

Put 1 tablespoon of sunflower oil in a small roasting tin (18cm square) and add 450g of sausages. Place the tin in a preheated oven at 220°C (425°F), Gas 7 for 10 minutes until the sausages are browned. Pour in the batter (see steps 1–2 of Yorkshire Pudding) and bake in the oven for 30–40 minutes until the batter is well risen and golden.

....

Pancakes

Makes 380ml and approximately 8 pancakes

115g plain wholemeal flour
pinch of salt
2 eggs
300ml milk
1–2 tbsp vegetable oil

Method

1. Put the flour and salt in a bowl and make a well in the centre. Break the eggs into the well. With a fork, start beating the mixture, gradually pulling flour in from around the well into the eggs until completely combined. Gradually add the milk and beat well to make a smooth batter.
2. Heat the oil in a frying pan, tilting the pan so that the oil spreads evenly.
3. When the pan is hot, pour in up to 2 tablespoons of batter, just enough to thinly coat the base. Tilt the pan so that the batter spreads evenly.
4. Cook over a medium heat until light-brown spots or flecks start

to appear on the underside of the pancake – this should only take 30–60 seconds. Slide a spatula under the pancake and flip it over to cook the other side.

5. Serve straightaway or transfer the pancakes to a plate as a stack with greaseproof paper in between each one, and keep warm.

....

Coating Batter

Makes 200ml

You will need a large frying pan

115g plain wholemeal flour
pinch of salt
1 egg
150ml milk (or milk and water)

Method

1. Sift the flour and salt into a bowl and make a well. Break in the egg and beat together well with a fork. Gradually add the milk to make a smooth batter. Dip your fruit, vegetable, fish or other candidate for battering into the mixture and then fry in a large frying pan for 2–3 minutes, turning once with a spatula, until golden brown.
2. Drain on kitchen paper and serve drizzled with honey.

Try using Coating Batter in Golden Banana Fritters (see page 22) or in Apple Fritters here. 400ml of the batter is needed for both recipes, so double the quantities.

Apple Fritters
Makes about 24

Retaining the skin, core 3 medium apples (preferably Bramley) and cut into rings about 0.5cm thick. Heat 1–2 tablespoons of sunflower oil in a large frying pan until hot, then dip each piece of apple in Coating Batter. Fry in the pan for 2–3 minutes, turning once with a spatula, until golden brown. Drain on kitchen paper and serve hot, drizzled with maple syrup or honey.

....

SAUCES

This basic white sauce is made with wholemeal flour and has a lovely nutty texture. It is made without a roux so contains less calories than most other white sauces.

Basic Béchamel Soup Base

This is not strictly béchamel, which is slightly more complex to make, not to mention full of butter. This is an easy and waistline -friendly alternative that can be used as a base for cream soups.

Makes 850ml, enough for 4 soup servings (see soup recipes on page 38)

850ml milk (or milk and water)
2 tbsp plain wholemeal flour

Method

1. In a large pan, gradually add 250ml of the milk to the flour and mix into a smooth paste with a wooden spoon.
2. Over a medium heat, gradually add a further 250ml of the milk while bringing the mixture slowly to the boil, stirring constantly.
3. Once the mixture has reached boiling point, reduce to a gentle simmer and gradually add the rest of the milk, stirring constantly. Simmer for a further 10 minutes.

Use Basic Béchamel Soup Base in Mackerel and Mushroom Chowder on page 45, Cream of Mushroom Soup on page 45, Cream of Celery Soup on page 44 and Spring Vegetable Soup on page 43.

Basic Béchamel Sauce

Again, not strictly béchamel sauce but a denser version of the Béchamel Soup Base to be used in pies, as a meat and vegetable sauce, and as a base for other sauces.

Makes 300ml

285ml milk
2 tbsp plain white flour

Method

1. Gradually add the milk to the flour in a saucepan and mix into a smooth paste with a wooden spoon.
2. Continue to stir as you bring the mixture to the boil.
3. Reduce the heat and cook for a further 10 minutes, stirring constantly.

Use Basic Béchamel Sauce as a base for Cheese Sauce on page 147 and Parsley Sauce on page 147, as well as in Savoury Pancakes on page 33, Root Vegetable Pie on page 57, Chicken and Sweetcorn Pie on page 97 and Streaky Bacon and Potato Pie on page 100.

Cheese Sauce

Makes 600ml, enough for 1 pie filling

115g grated Cheddar cheese
1 tsp mustard powder or mustard
600ml Basic Béchamel Sauce (see 146) – do not allow to cool
        as the cheese needs to be able to melt in the sauce
sea salt and freshly ground black pepper

Method

Add the cheese and mustard powder to the béchamel sauce and
season to taste with salt and pepper. Stir until thoroughly blended.

*Use Cheese Sauce in Layered Red Lentil, Spinach and Potato Casserole
on page 49.*

Parsley Sauce

Makes 600ml. Good with white fish fillets

600ml Basic Béchamel Sauce (see page 146)
3 level tbsp finely chopped flat-leaf parsley
1–2 tsp white wine vinegar (optional)
sea salt and freshly ground black pepper

Method

Season the béchamel sauce with salt and pepper and stir in the finely
chopped parsley immediately before serving. When serving parsley
sauce with fish, add 1–2 teaspoons of white wine vinegar for
a piquant flavour.

Creole Brown Sauce

Makes 300ml, served with fish fillets

1 tbsp grated onion
1 tbsp grated garlic
45g butter
85g plain white flour
100ml single cream
100ml full-fat milk
1 tsp Marmite or Vegemite
pinch of chilli powder
sea salt and freshly ground black pepper

Method

1. In a large saucepan, brown the onion and garlic in the butter over a medium heat, stirring for 3–5 minutes until soft.
2. Gradually stir in the flour. Slowly add the cream, milk and 100ml of cold water, stirring constantly with a wooden spoon until slightly thickened – this should take about 3–5 minutes.
3. Season with the Marmite or Vegemite, salt, pepper and chilli powder and cook for 2–3 minutes until you have a spicy brown sauce.

....

Tomato Sauce

Makes about 300ml, enough for 4. Serve with pasta

1 tbsp vegetable oil
2 onions, finely chopped
1 garlic clove, crushed
1 tsp mixed herbs
400g tin of tomatoes
1 tsp soy sauce

1 tsp soft light brown sugar
1 tbsp tomato purée
sea salt and freshly ground black pepper

Method

1. Heat the oil in a saucepan and gently fry the onions with the garlic and mixed herbs for 5 minutes.
2. Add the tinned tomatoes, crushing them with a wooden spoon.
3. Season with salt and pepper and stir in the soy sauce, brown sugar and tomato purée.
4. Cover and simmer gently for 30–45 minutes.

Mint Sauce

Makes enough for 6–8. Serve with roast lamb

1–2 tbsp caster sugar
pinch of salt
bunch of mint leaves, chopped
4–5 tbsp white wine vinegar

Method

Dissolve the sugar and salt in 50ml of boiling water, add the chopped mint and vinegar and stir well.

Apple Sauce

Makes about 200ml, enough for 4. Serve with roast pork

450g Bramley apples, cored and sliced
20g butter
squeeze of lemon juice (optional)

Method

1. Put the apples in an uncovered saucepan with 2–3 tablespoons of cold water and cook on a low-medium heat for about 10 minutes until soft.
2. Mash to a pulp with a wooden spoon and stir in the butter. Continue to stir until the butter has completely melted. Add a squeeze of lemon juice if using up eating apples.

....

Egg Preparations

Soft-boiled

1. Place 4 eggs and 1 teaspoon of white vinegar in a pan of cold salted water, enough to cover the eggs, and bring to the boil.
2. Reduce the heat and simmer gently for 2–3 minutes, then plunge the eggs into cold water.

Hard-boiled

1. Place 4 eggs in a simmering pan of salted water with 1 teaspoon of white vinegar. Allow to simmer for 10 minutes, then place them under cold running water.
2. Tap the shells and leave them to cool. Once cool, crack the shell all over and peel off.

Tip for hard-boiling eggs

Eggs lowered into simmering water are more likely to have their yolks in the centre than those put into cold water. To avoid a dark ring around the yolk, do not over-boil.

Coddled

By definition, coddled eggs are partially cooked and for that reason you should endeavour to use the freshest eggs possible. Specialised egg coddlers can be used, but coddled eggs can also be made while still in their shells.

1. Place 4 eggs in a pan of boiling water with 1 teaspoon of white vinegar, cover and remove from the heat.
2. Leave for 10 minutes, then serve.

Poached

As with coddled eggs, use the freshest eggs you can get hold of.

1. Bring to a simmer a medium-size pan half filled with lightly salted water. Add 1 teaspoon of white vinegar to the water.
2. Break the eggs one at a time into lightly greased cups and slip gently into the simmering water, season with salt and pepper, cover the pan with a lid and reduce the heat.
3. Cook gently over a low heat until the eggs have set – this should take about 2½–3 minutes – then lift them out with a slotted spoon.

Scrambled

Feeds 4

1. Warm 30g of butter in a saucepan over a low heat until just beginning to melt. Remove the pan from the heat and allow it to cool slightly.
2. Break 6 eggs straight into the pan with 1 teaspoon each of milk and salt. Beat with a wooden spoon until smooth.
3. Return the pan to the lowest heat setting, stirring constantly for 5–10 minutes until the mixture is creamily set. Sprinkle with freshly ground black pepper and serve immediately.

Baked

You will need 1 ramekin per baked egg

1. Preheat the oven to 180°C (350°F), Gas 4.
2. Put a tiny knob of butter in each ramekin and place the ramekins in the oven as it is warming up, just long enough to allow the butter to melt. Once the butter has melted, break 1 egg into each ramekin.

3. Season with salt and pepper and bake in the oven for 8–10 minutes until the eggs are just set. Serve the eggs in the ramekins.

Fried

Melt a little butter or vegetable oil in a frying pan. Break each egg separately into a cup and slide into the hot fat. Cook gently for 1–2 minutes over a low heat, basting with the fat, until set. Remove with a spatula and serve.

....

Omelette

Feeds 2. Makes 1 large omelette

You will need a medium frying pan, approximately 25cm across

6 eggs
30g butter
sea salt and freshly ground black pepper

Method

1. Crack the eggs into a bowl and add 1 tablespoon of cold water (I use water instead of milk to prevent the omelette from becoming rubbery). Beat the mixture with a fork for 30 seconds. Season with salt and pepper.
2. Melt the butter in a frying pan over a medium heat, but don't let it brown or the omelette may stick.
3. Pour in the egg mixture once the butter starts to sizzle.
4. Wait for the mixture to set slightly, then draw the edges into the centre with the back of a fork or a spatula so the uncooked egg can run into the space. Continue until the egg is almost set, about 3–4 minutes. Cook on no higher than a medium heat to stop the omelette from becoming tough.
5. Stop stirring and allow it to brown lightly on the bottom.

When cooked underneath but still soft on top, turn over a third of your omelette into the centre, then fold over the opposite third.
6. Turn out onto a warm plate.

Tips for omelettes

If you're a fan of omelettes, keep a special pan for omelette-making and wipe out with paper towels after use to preserve an oily surface. Ideally, omelette pans should be small to medium (about 20–25cm across), light enough to handle, and have slanted edges to allow your omelette to slide out easily after cooking.

....

Homemade Yoghurt

To make your own yoghurt you will need a little bought live yoghurt to start you off. After that you can use your homemade yoghurt. There's no need for a yoghurt maker, a heavy glass casserole dish or earthenware pot with a lid can be used in a warm oven or airing cupboard. Alternatively, a thermos flask can be used. Ensure that any equipment used is squeaky clean and dry before making your yoghurt.

Feeds 4, makes 570ml

570ml full-fat milk
2 tbsp natural probiotic yoghurt at room temperature

Method

1. Bring the milk almost to the boil, stirring constantly.
2. Leave the milk to cool, still stirring to ensure the temperature is even throughout, until it is warm but not hot. If you can hold your little finger in the milk for 10 seconds without it burning, that's about right.
3. Stir in the yoghurt, cover and leave in a warm oven at around 55°C (110°F) or in a warm airing cupboard for 3–6 hours.

Try not to move the container during this period or the yoghurt will separate. Alternatively, pour into a warm thermos flask and leave overnight.

4. Once set, pour the yoghurt into containers with lids and put in the fridge until cool, then your yoghurt is ready to eat.

Yoghurt tips

For a creamier batch, substitute half the milk for single cream or add 1 tablespoon of skimmed milk powder.

Add fruit and other flavours, such as vanilla essence, just before serving.

Delicious in drinks, dressings, dips and breakfast cereals – try Healthy Honey–Yoghurt Sundae (see page 23).

Cast-Iron Frying Pan with Lid

There is one item I could never do without and that is my cast-iron frying pan with a lid. It's the most useful of all my pans – excellent for sautéeing, stir-fries and stews, it's sturdy and hard-wearing. I've had mine for over 30 years. In fact, I have two cast-iron frying pans – one for savouries and one for sweets.

Care of your cast-iron pan

It's important after using a frying pan for cooking meat, fish or strong-smelling dishes like curry to wash and rinse it thoroughly. After that, it helps to wipe it with a clean cloth then dry it over a low heat. Add 1 tablespoon of oil and tilt the pan so that the oil spreads around. This prevents the pan from rusting.

BERNIE'S GOOD BUDGET GUIDE

To help you slash your food bills further, here's Bernie's Good Budget Guide – a quick and handy reference section, with tips and suggestions guaranteed to save you money and help you become a savvy shopper.

BERNIE'S TOP SHOPPING TIPS

- Make a shopping list before going grocery shopping and stick to it.

- Plan weekly shopping and menus around ingredients you already have in stock.

- Check the prices of the items on your shopping list online to cost it up.

- Only put the amount you wish to spend in your purse so you're not tempted to splurge.

○ A little extra could be kept in the shopping purse for genuine bargains only, enabling you to save in the long run.

○ Use cash – shopping with a credit card encourages you to spend more on things you don't need.

○ Only buy bargains you really need. Nothing is cheap if you do not want it.

○ Shop around; it's easy to check online what promotions are on offer.

○ Take advantage of seasonal promotions.

○ Catch market bargains at the end of the day.

○ Catch supermarket bargains before closing time, especially before holiday closing times.

○ Don't go for expensive brands in supermarkets, the food is not necessarily of a better quality.

○ Be sure that a 'reduced' item on offer is genuinely reduced.

○ Make a note when supplies of anything are running low. This should help reduce the number of shopping trips you take.

○ Don't shop when you are hungry.

○ Don't buy too many perishable ingredients at once. Buy only what you need when shopping for fresh food.

○ Find a good, local butcher for fresh, seasonal produce and buy cheap cuts like beef rib, pork loin, hand of pork, lamb shank and breast of lamb.

○ Make more than one meal from one main ingredient – for example, 1 hand of pork (lower part of the pork shoulder) can make a slow pot roast, sandwiches, stew, a pie, and soup.

○ It's cheaper to buy a whole chicken than chicken pieces.

○ Fruit and vegetables are usually cheaper and fresher from a market than from a supermarket.

○ It's cheaper to buy fruit and vegetables whole rather than pre-chopped, and they retain more of their nutritional value whole, too.

○ Always check the 'use by' dates when buying food, so you don't have to throw it out the next day.

○ Use money-off coupons where possible – found in magazines, supermarket publications, newspaper promotions and discount websites featuring 'deals of the day'.

○ Check and keep all food receipts. Receipts can be calculated on a daily or weekly basis to see how much you're spending on food. Keep receipts in case you need to return unsatisfactory products.

○ Make sure all BOGOFs and other promotions have been included on receipts (sometimes mistakes are made and promotions have not been counted).

○ Don't be afraid to inform staff if you have been overcharged.

○ Don't use a trolley when shopping, carry a basket – the bigger the trolley, the more you fill it.

○ Don't fall for the trick red-label promotions without checking first that a bargain really is on offer.

○ Get the kids on your side when shopping and teach them how to shop – they can help with arithmetic!

A SEASON FOR EVERYTHING

Eating food that is in season and has been produced locally is the way forward for all of us and is better.

Why?

Better taste and more nutrients: Seasonal fruit and vegetables grown in the conditions to which they are best suited are firmer, have more flavour and have a higher nutritional value than those that aren't.

Better planet: Eating local, seasonal food cuts down on food miles and carbon emissions caused by transporting food from around the world, helping us to achieve a low-impact lifestyle. Fresh food also has less packaging, creates less domestic waste and is more sustainable.

Better price: Buying fresh, local produce is much cheaper in relative terms than buying food flown from the other side of the world. Local markets are the best place to shop for price and variety. Buying locally also helps support your local community.

More variety: Eating seasonally means having a regular change of menu. Cooking food in season also encourages creativity in the kitchen and a change of cooking habits, banishing dull mealtime routines.

SEASONAL FOOD CALENDAR

January

Fruit: pippin apples, pears, forced rhubarb.

Vegetables: aubergines, beetroot, broccoli, Brussels sprouts, cabbage, carrots, cauliflower, celeriac, celery, garlic, kale, leeks, mushrooms, onions, parsnips, potatoes, shallots, spinach (winter), squash, turnips, swede.

Fish: haddock, mussels, plaice, herring, shrimps.

Meat: beef, chicken, mutton, pork, turkey.

February

Fruit: golden pippin apples, golden russet apples, pears, forced rhubarb.

Vegetables: beet, broccoli, Brussels sprouts, cabbage, carrots, cauliflower, celery, chicory, kale, leeks, mushrooms, onions, parsnips, potatoes, shallots, spinach, squash, swede, turnips.

Fish: cockles, haddock, herring, mussels, shrimps.

Meat: beef, chicken, mutton, pork, turkey.

March

Fruit: golden pippin apples, golden russet apples, pears, pomegranates, rhubarb.

Vegetables: beetroot, broccoli, Brussels sprouts, cabbage, carrots, cauliflower, garlic, leeks, mint, onions, parsley, parsnips, potatoes, radishes, spinach, turnips.

Fish: cockles, herring, mackerel, mussels, pilchards, prawns, sardines, shrimps.

Meat: beef, chicken, mutton, pork, turkey.

April

Fruit: apples, pears, rhubarb.

Vegetables: asparagus, broccoli, cabbage, carrots, cauliflower, cucumber, fennel, kale, lettuce, onions, parsley, parsnips, peas, potatoes, radishes, spinach, watercress.

Fish: haddock, herring, mackerel, mussels, pilchards, prawns, sardines, shrimp.

Meat: beef, chicken, mutton, pork, spring lamb, turkey.

May

Fruit: apples, cherries, gooseberries, pears, rhubarb.

Vegetables: asparagus, beetroot, broccoli, broad beans, cabbage, carrots, cauliflower, celery, cucumber, fennel, garlic, leeks, lettuce, mint, mushrooms, onions, parsley, peas, new potatoes, radishes, rocket, spinach, spring onions, turnips, watercress.

Fish: herring, mackerel, mullet, pilchards, prawns, sardines, shrimps.

Meat: beef, chicken, lamb, mutton, pork, turkey.

June

Fruit: apples, cherries, gooseberries, pears, raspberries, redcurrants, rhubarb, strawberries, tomatoes.

Vegetables: asparagus, aubergines, beetroot, broad beans, cabbage, carrots, cauliflower, courgettes, cucumber, leeks, lettuce, onions, peas, peppers, potatoes, spinach, turnips, marrows.

Fish: herring, mackerel, mullet, pilchards, prawns, sardines, shrimps.

Meat: beef, chicken, mutton, pork, turkey, Welsh lamb.

July

Fruit: apples, blueberries, cherries, gooseberries, greengages, pears, plums, raspberries, redcurrants, rhubarb, strawberries, tomatoes.

Vegetables: asparagus, aubergines, beetroot, broad beans, cabbage, carrots, cauliflower, celery, courgettes, cucumber, lettuce, mushrooms, peas, peppers, potatoes, radishes, runner beans, spinach, turnips.

Fish: crab, herring, mackerel, pilchards, prawns, shrimp, trout.

Meat: beef, lamb, mutton.

August

Fruit: apples, blackberries, cherries, figs, gooseberries, greengages, loganberries, mulberries, pears, plums, raspberries, redcurrants, strawberries, tomatoes.

Vegetables: aubergines, basil, carrots, cauliflower, celery, courgettes, cucumber, fennel, leeks, lettuce, mushrooms, onions, peas, peppers, potatoes, radishes, runner beans, spinach, sweetcorn.

Fish: herring, mackerel, mullet, prawns, shrimps, trout.

Meat: beef, lamb, mutton.

September

Fruit: apples, blackberries, cherries, damsons, elderberries, figs, grapes, hazelnuts, mulberries, peaches, pears, plums, raspberries, rhubarb, strawberries, tomatoes.

Vegetables: aubergines, cabbage, carrots, cauliflower, celery, cucumber, runner beans, kale, leeks, lettuce, mushrooms, onions, parsnips, peas, peppers, potatoes, pumpkin, radishes, spinach, sweetcorn.

Fish: cockles, hake, herring, mackerel, mullet, mussels, shrimp, whiting.

Meat: beef, chicken, mutton, pork, turkey.

October

Fruit: apples, blackberries, cranberries, elderberries, figs, hazelnuts, mulberries, pears, tomatoes.

Vegetables: aubergines, beetroot, broccoli, cabbage, carrots, cauliflower, courgettes, kale, leek, lettuce, marrow, mushrooms, onions, parsnips, peas, potatoes, pumpkin, radishes, runner beans, spinach, squash, turnips, watercress.

Fish: cockles, hake, herring, mackerel, mussels, shrimps.

Meat: beef, chicken, mutton, pork, turkey.

November

Fruit: apples, chestnuts, cranberries, hazelnuts, pears.

Vegetables: beetroot, broccoli, Brussels sprouts, cabbage, carrots, cauliflower, celery, leeks, onions, parsnips, potatoes, pumpkin, spinach, swede, turnips.

Fish: cockles, hake, herring, mackerel, mussels, shrimps.

Meat: beef, chicken, mutton, pork, turkey.

December

Fruit: apples, chestnuts, hazelnuts, pears, pomegranate, rhubarb.

Vegetables: beetroot, broccoli, Brussels sprouts, cabbage, carrots, cauliflower, celery, onions, parsnips, potatoes, pumpkin, red cabbage, spinach, swede, turnips.

Fish: hake, herring, mussels, shrimps, sprats.

Meat: beef, chicken, goose, lamb, mutton, pork, turkey.

USES FOR LEFTOVER INGREDIENTS

Apples
Use up old apples in sweet and sour stir-fries, apple sauce, crumbles, salads, cereals and puddings.

Pears
Poach in leftover wine, use in smoothies, sauces, syrups and sorbets.

Oranges and lemons
Use up old oranges and lemons in marinades, sauces and sorbets.

Bananas
Overripe bananas can be peeled and chopped into three, bagged and frozen for use in smoothies, pancakes, puddings, muffins and bread.

Carrots
Can be used in cakes, smoothies, salads, stir-fries, soups, stews, flans, stocks and sauces.

Tomatoes
Sauces, salsas, stir-fries, pizza toppings, soups, juices, risottos, with bacon and baked with beans.

Onions
Soups, stews, sauces, pies, casseroles, pizzas, salads, stocks or for caramelising (sauté in a drop of oil, add a little sugar and stir-fry until brown and thickened).

Bread
Make breadcrumbs or Bread and Butter Pudding. Freeze sliced bread and use for toast. Freeze half a large loaf and use later in the week.

Cakes and biscuits
Leftover cakes and biscuits can be used up in flan cases, puddings, crumbles and trifles.

Wine, beer or cider

Freeze leftover wine, beer or cider in ice-cube trays to use in sauces.

Juice pulp

Make stock with pulp from the juicer and use in soups, stews, cakes and muffins. Freeze fruit pulp with lemon or orange juice to make sorbet cubes, freeze with yoghurt, mix with ice cream, use in cake and muffins. Use vegetable pulp in meat loaf, veggie burgers, flans and pies.

Cooking juices

Use a jar with a screw lid as a stock jug to collect leftover juices from cooking and keep in the fridge for up to 4 days.

- Freeze leftover ingredients to use in pies, burgers, omelettes and stir-fries etc.
- Bag leftover meals and freeze to use as 'ready meals'.
- Cooked food can be puréed and frozen on the day of cooking for infant meals, being careful to make sure that no salt is added.

HEALTHY EATING GUIDE

- Enjoy your food. Eat a variety of fresh food in season.
- Try to substitute some of the food made with refined white flour with bread, pasta, wholegrain rice and cereals.
- Snack on nuts, seeds, fruit and vegetables.
- Have a side salad of seasonal vegetables with your main meal each day.
- Boost your fruit and vegetable intake with freshly made soup, smoothies and juices.
- Eat oily fish like mackerel, sardines and herring twice a week for Omegas 3 and 6.
- Eat the skin of potatoes and apples for Vitamin C and fibre.
- Soft margarine is high in polyunsaturates and low in saturated fat, so try to use it where you would usually use butter.

- Try substituting mayonnaise for Greek yoghurt, which has only a fraction of the fat content and calories.
- Use crème fraîche or Greek yoghurt in mashed potatoes or vegetables.
- Boost your immune system with fresh herbs, chilli, garlic, ginger and spices.
- Drink 1 cup of water or herbal tea every 2 hours to rehydrate your brain and body.
- Cut down on caffeine, alcohol and fizzy drinks.

MORE TOP TIPS

- Make minced meat go further by adding lentils, soya mince or chopped vegetables.
- Fine oatmeal is good for bulking out meals like burgers and meat loaf to make them go further.
- Cook lentils and beans in bulk and freeze in their cooking liquid for quick stir-fries, and curries.
- Stock-take regularly – check which foods need using up, especially those hidden in the back of the fridge.
- Have at least one main meal per week using up leftover ingredients; see what delicious concoctions you can create.
- Bake your own bread and rolls and make your own packed lunches.
- Freeze food you will not be able to consume before its 'use by' date.
- Freeze food once only and make sure meat and fish thaw completely before cooking.
- Reheat food once only and cook thoroughly at a high temperature to kill off any bacteria.
- Keep all stored food in sealed containers and allow food to cool fully before refrigerating.
- To prevent cross-contamination, do not put cooked meat next to uncooked meat.

- Keep food on the fridge shelf that corresponds to its ideal temperature to prevent it from going off.
- Wrap meat and fish before storing at the bottom of the fridge, and store dairy produce at the top.
- To keep the fridge smelling fresh, wrap up any onions or garlic before storing inside.
- Freshen up your fridge and cupboards with the zest of oranges and lemons.
- Never leave cooked food out of the fridge for more than 90 minutes.
- Wash your hands regularly when preparing food and especially after touching other items.
- Cover any cuts, burns or abrasions on your hands when cooking.
- Wash your hands after preparing fresh chillies to prevent burning contact with the eyes or any other body part.
- Remove any food smells on hands and chopping boards with lemon juice, then rinse.
- Clean surfaces and equipment thoroughly after use, especially after preparing chicken.
- Save on the washing up by lining baking tins and grill pans with foil.
- To reduce mess, use minimum utensils when cooking and clear up as you go along.
- Keep bins clean, covered and away from any food preparation areas.
- An orange studded with cloves keeps the kitchen smelling naturally fresh.
- Grow your own fruit, vegetables and herbs.
- Make your own compost from teabags and fruit and vegetable peelings.

WEEKLY MEAL PLANNER

Week One

	Breakfast	Lunch	Dinner
Sun	Toasted Oats with Raisins, Bananas and Strawberries	Mackerel Pâté Sandwiches	Honey-Roast Chicken, Roast Potatoes & Crisp Green Salad
Mon	Honey Polenta	Roast Chicken and Salad Sandwiches	Sautéed Onion, Tomato and Red Split Lentil Tart, Chunky Oven Chips & Salad
Tues	Grilled Banana Split	Savoury Pancakes	Roast Chicken and Chunky Vegetable Soup with Butter Dumplings
Wed	Perfect Creamy Porridge	Gourmet Sardines on Toast	Healthy Black-Eyed Beanburgers, Jacket Potatoes & Decadent Winter Slaw
Thur	Scrambled Eggs on Toast	Minestrone	Chilli Prawns in Coconut Cream, Brown Rice & Crunchy Red Bean and Green Pepper Salad
Fri	Healthy Honey-Yoghurt Sundae	Spicy Winter Bean Stew	Cheddar and Sautéed Onion Quiche, Jacket Potatoes & Vibrant Carrot, Raisin and Rice Salad
Sat	Honey Popcorn	Welsh Rarebit	Stir-Fried Liver with Ginger, Buttery Mash & Peas

Week Two

	Breakfast	Lunch	Dinner
Sun	Perfect Creamy Porridge	Savoury Bread and Cheese Pudding	Slow-Roast Shoulder of Pork with Apple, Buttery Mash & Steamed Broccoli
Mon	Breakfast Corncake Stack	Roast Pork Sandwiches	Cheesy Sweet Potato and Bean Bake, Creole Brown Sauce & Steamed Carrots
Tues	Honey Polenta	Omelette with Sautéed Mushrooms	Autumnal Black–Eyed Bean Stew with Dumplings
Wed	Healthy Honey-Yoghurt Sundae	Tuna and Sweetcorn Sandwiches	Wholemeal Cream Cheese and Vine Tomato Pizza, Jacket Potatoes & Sweet Potato Salad with a Lemon Honey Dressing
Thur	Peanut Butter and Date Granola	Tomato Bouillon & Farmhouse Cheese and Potato Cakes	Mushroom-Stuffed Mackerel, Brown Rice & Crunchy Red Bean and Green Pepper Salad
Fri	Scrambled Eggs on Toast	Crispy Potato Fritters	Spaghetti Neapolitan & Crisp Green Salad
Sat	Grilled Banana Split	Marinated Mackerel with Fresh Greens and a Zingy Mustard Dressing	Creole Corn-Crust Chicken, Buttery Mash & Peas

Week Three

	Breakfast	Lunch	Dinner
Sun	Golden Apricot Granola	Scrambled Eggs and Smoked Salmon	Potato, Cheddar and Onion Tart with Spring Greens & Salad
Mon	Fruit and Nut Breakfast Trail Mix	Baked Beans on Toast	Sweet Potato, Coriander and Chilli Fishcakes, Steamed Cauliflower & Brown Rice
Tues	Grilled Banana Split	Cheese Omelette	Red Pepper Risotto and Crisp Green Salad
Wed	Toasted Oats with Raisins, Bananas and Strawberries	Minestrone	Red Beanburgers, Baked Potato and Crispy Green Salad
Thur	Healthy Honey-Yoghurt Sundae	Smoked Mackerel on Toast	Ham and Mushroom Wholewheat Spaghetti in Tomato Sauce & Crisp Green Salad
Fri	Perfect Creamy Porridge	Sautéed Mushroom, Onion and Beansprout Pancakes	Mama's Pan Chicken, Brown Rice & The Original Potato Salad
Sat	Honey Polenta	Welsh Rarebit	Sautéed Onion, Tomato and Red Split Lentil Tart, Jacket Potatoes & Decadent Winter Slaw

Week Four

	Breakfast	Lunch	Dinner
Sun	Popcorn for Breakfast	Scrambled Eggs on Toast	Caribbean Spiced Lamb Shanks, Roast Potatoes & Steamed Green Beans
Mon	Toasted Oats with Raisins, Bananas and Strawberries	Roast Lamb Butties	Red Pepper Risotto & Crisp Green Salad
Tues	Grilled Banana Split	Spring Vegetable Soup	Sweet Potato Coriander and Chilli Fishcakes
Wed	Perfect Creamy Porridge	Savoury Pancakes	Rich Chicken and Mixed Vegetable Curry
Thur	Heidi Breakfast	Potato Fritters	Rustic Kidney Bean, Green Pepper and Mushroom Goulash, Brown Rice & Crisp Green Salad
Fri	Honey Polenta	Mackerel Pâté on Toast	Streaky Bacon and Potato Pie, Steamed Carrots & Creole Brown Sauce
Sat	Scrambled Eggs with Smoked Salmon	Warming Cheesy Rice Bake	Crispy Fish Fillets, Chunky Oven Chips & Salad

INDEX

INDEX